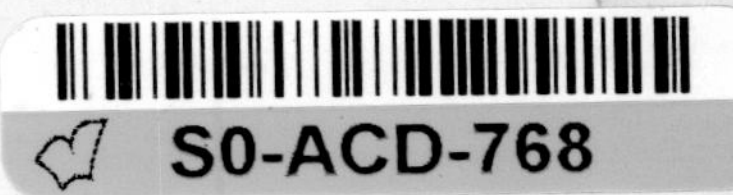
S0-ACD-768

Eastern Religions

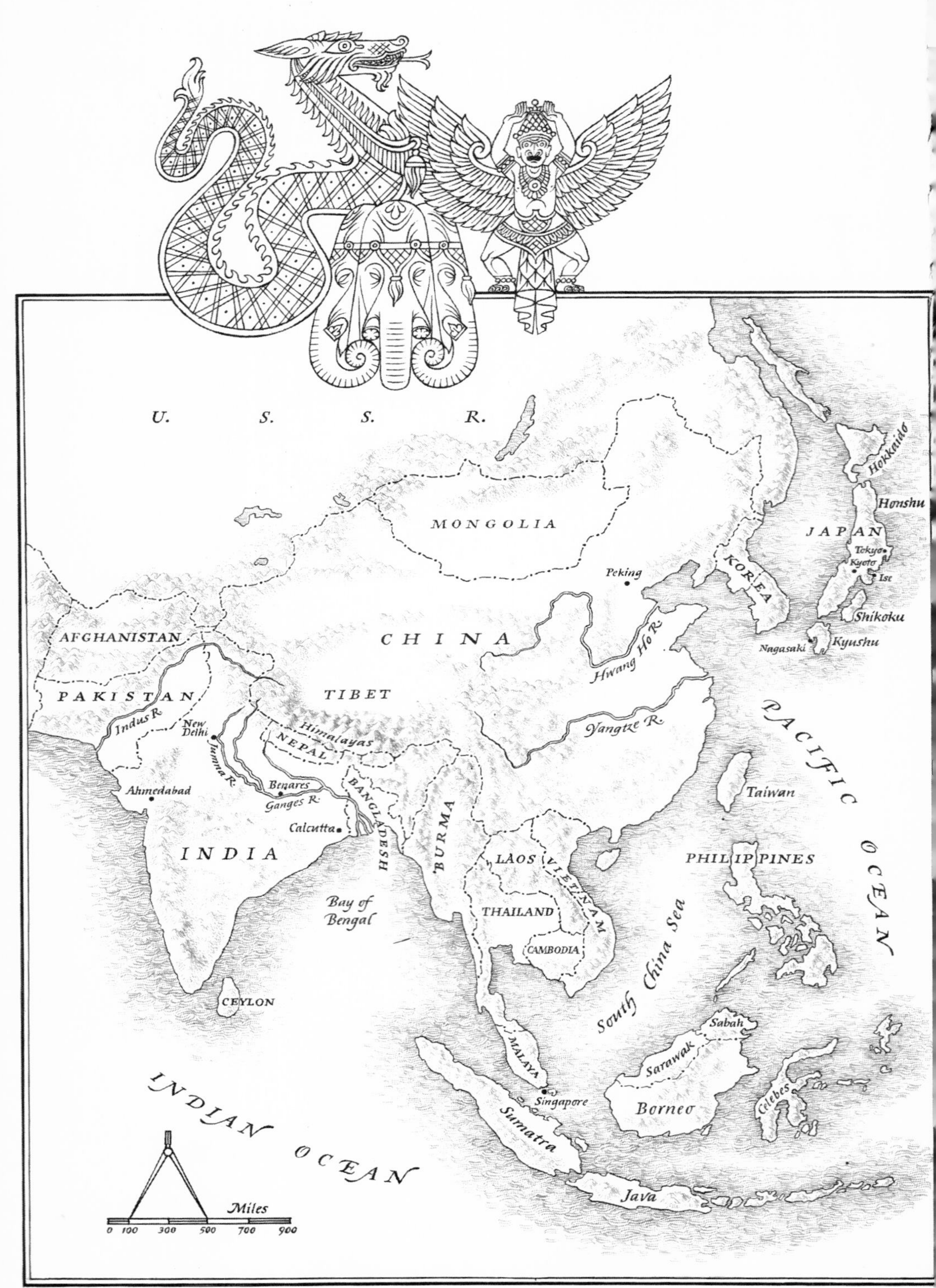

U. S. S. R.
MONGOLIA
Peking
KOREA
JAPAN
Hokkaido
Honshu
Tokyo
Kyoto
Ise
Shikoku
Kyushu
Nagasaki
AFGHANISTAN
CHINA
Hwang Ho R.
PAKISTAN
TIBET
Indus R.
New Delhi
Himalayas
NEPAL
Yangtze R.
PACIFIC OCEAN
Jumna R.
Benares
Ganges R.
Ahmedabad
BANGLADESH
Taiwan
Calcutta
BURMA
INDIA
LAOS
VIETNAM
PHILIPPINES
Bay of Bengal
THAILAND
CAMBODIA
South China Sea
CEYLON
Sabah
MALAYA
Sarawak
Singapore
Borneo
Celebes
Sumatra
INDIAN OCEAN
Java
Miles
0 100 300 500 700 900

Eastern Religions

by ELIZABETH SEEGER

Illustrated with Photographs

Thomas Y. Crowell Company New York

Published simultaneously in Canada by Fitzhenry & Whiteside Limited, Toronto.

Designed by Sallie Baldwin

Manufactured in the United States of America

ISBN 0-690-25342-7

1 2 3 4 5 6 7 8 9 10

Library of Congress Cataloging in Publication Data

Seeger, Elizabeth.
Eastern religions.
Bibliography: p.
SUMMARY: Introduces the history, philosophies, and rituals of such Eastern religions as Hinduism, Buddhism, Shintoism, Confucianism, and Taoism.
1. Asia—Religion—Juv. lit. [1. Asia—Religion. 2. Religions] I. Title. BL92.S43 294 73-10206 ISBN 0-690-25342-7

Contents

Pronunciation of Foreign Words

As a general rule:

a = *ah,* as in f*a*ther
e = *e,* as in s*e*t
ei = *ay,* as in r*ei*n
i = *ee,* as in pol*i*ce
o = *o,* as in h*o*le
u = *u,* as in r*u*le
ai = *y,* as in cr*y*
ao or au = *ow,* as in n*ow*

In Chinese words the consonants are usually softened: Tao = *dow;* chou = *jo;* tse = *dze.* The final *e* is hardly pronounced at all; the only approximate sound in English is the *e* in th*e.*

In Indian words there is no *th,* as in too*th.* The *t* and the *h* are separate, as in foo*th*old. The Buddha's given name is pronounced Sidd-hart-ha. The unaccented *a*'s are pronounced as they are in English: the two *a*'s in Gótama are like the two final *a*'s in Can*a*d*a.*

Eastern Religions

A view of the Himalayas. *(By Deane Dickason from Ewing Galloway, New York)*

PART ONE

East and West

All the great religions of the world have come from Asia. Judaism, Christianity, and Islam (the religion taught by Muhammad) are closely related and come from the extreme western part of the continent where the Semitic people first lived. Hinduism and Buddhism come from India; Confucianism and Taoism from China; and there are other faiths, less well known outside their own countries, such as Shinto in Japan. These can be called the great religions because they have held the belief of many millions of people and have remained vital, some for thousands of years, some for less. Judaism, Christianity, and Islam belong both to the East and to the West. This book is concerned with those that belong primarily to the East: those of India, China, and Japan.

East and West, with capital letters, are somewhat

vague terms. In this book, as in many others, the East denotes the lands and the nations of Asia while the West denotes those of Europe and all the other parts of the world that are possessed and governed by Europeans or by their descendants: North and South America, Australia, parts of Africa and many other places. The two terms are cultural rather than geographical; for example, Siberia is in Asia but belongs to the West, since it is possessed and governed by the Russians.

The people of the West, then, have received their faith from other races; they have not thought it out themselves. They, and especially we in America, have received it, too, from great distances and at several removes; for we have been migrants, moving ever westward, for many centuries. We are separated, beyond hope of return, from the roots of our religion, from the land where it had its birth.

We have lost, in the process, an intuitive communion with the earth and the forces of nature which all people know in the very early days of their history and which is usually a vital part of their religion. For they perceive a power greater than themselves, but at first they are unable to understand the whole, and worship it in part: as sun and moon, as wind and fire, as earth and sky. And if they remain in their homeland, they do not entirely lose that communion, even when they become civilized and their belief becomes more mature. It is, indeed, a precious thing. In America, only the Indian can know it, for the people from all parts of the world who have flooded the two continents had lost it long before they came here or have left it behind them in distant countries. The individual may deeply love his adopted land, but the communal festivals and rituals that celebrate the seasons, the planting and the harvesting, the phases of sun and moon, are not easily transported.

The peoples of eastern Asia have stayed where they

first settled as primitive, nomadic tribes. The Aryans came into India, thousands of years ago, from the same place where the Europeans started their long westward migration. There is no proof or tradition of any immigration into China. As far as they know, the Chinese have always lived on their rich, coastal plain, nourished by its great rivers and protected, as they believed, by their holy mountains. The Japanese have an even closer relation with their beautiful islands, for islands are more separate and more self-contained than continental lands and their people know them even more intimately because, in the early days, they knew no other place.

This communion with nature is present in all the religions we are concerned with. The memory of the early gods remains even after philosophers and great religious leaders have attained the highest degree of spiritual understanding.

From the beginning of civilization, all over the world, men have asked themselves, as they faced the terrors and the wonders that surrounded them, "Where did this universe come from?" "How was it made and what is it made of?" "What is man and what is his part in it?" "And death? Is life finished when the body dies?" When we ask ourselves these and other questions, as we still do, we have a vast store of knowledge and of speculation to draw upon. But there was a time when there was no previous knowledge, no books, and no teachers. The questions had to be answered by those who asked them. Some of the greatest men in the world's history gave their lives to the solving of these problems and have left us their findings. We shall do well to listen to them, for their answers form the basis of all religions and are at the foundation of the different cultures of mankind.

The answers are very much alike, for all peoples have

recognized a spiritual presence and power that we call God. They believe that there is a relationship between man and God that is very important for man's welfare and happiness, and they are convinced that this relation depends upon the way man lives and behaves. The moral codes, written and unwritten, which are an important part of every faith, are based on this conviction.

There are also differences, for races and nations vary as much—and as little—as individuals do. For example, in the Western world the idea of God is a personal one: God is a male figure, a father, loving and watching over his creation, of which mankind is held to be the most important part. Of course, there are almost as many ideas of God as there are people, and many, both in the East and the West, do not believe in God at all. Nevertheless, this is the image that is presented in the Bible and that permeates our religious life.

In the East different ideas are found. The Indians, whose religion has been the most influential there, think of God as impersonal, absolute, beyond the reach of words or of any description, for description is a limitation and God cannot be limited. Words must be used, of course, for nothing can be talked about without them, and the Hindus give many names to God: "Brahman," "the Self," "Absolute Being, Knowledge, and Bliss." But they know that these are makeshifts, and in one of the most important statements of their scriptures God is simply "That." For they have a great longing for what is infinite and unchanging, for unity in the midst of the multitude of ever-changing appearances of our world. To the Hindu believer this Absolute Being, which is "within all and without all," is the true reality, far more real than the world that our senses perceive. It can be known only by the intuition, which is an inner realization and conviction, independent of thought and reason. To most Western people the world is real, and reason is more to be trusted than intuition. Both are indispensable faculties of the human mind.

In China, too, the name of God is Heaven, the Great Unity, the Way, the Nameless. All through the East, in its beliefs, its arts, its ways of living, one finds this distinction between the finite and the infinite, the real and the unreal, the world of the "opposites"—birth and death, good and bad, dark and light, joy and sorrow—and the all-pervading, transcendent world of the spirit.

It appears in Japan because many Japanese have turned to Buddhism, which comes from India. But Shinto, their original faith, lays more stress upon the finite than upon the infinite. The Shintoist recognizes the same spiritual presence that other religions do and finds it everywhere; but to him the material world is very real and desirable and he celebrates it in many delightful ways.

The differences and the similarities in the cultures of the world make an absorbing study. Nowhere are the differences more interesting and the similarities more important than in the field of religion. "God is One," said a Hindu saint, "but He is worshiped in different ages and climes under different names and aspects."[1]

The great Hindu temple at Tanjore. *(Government of India Tourist Office)*

PART TWO

Hinduism

Lead us from the unreal to the Real;
From darkness into Light;
From death into Immortality!

—from the Vedas

When the Aryans came into northern India, probably about 2000 B.C., they came over the northwestern passes through which most of the conquerors of India have traveled. They moved slowly, for they were herdsmen and farmers and, as they traveled, they must feed their families and their cattle and therefore stayed for years in one place before moving on to another. They settled first in the Punjab, the Land of the Five Rivers: those which flow into the great river Indus. Still more slowly they moved across the northern plains and into the valley of the other great river, the Ganges, that flows into the Bay of Bengal. They settled in villages, farming and pasturing their herds on the rich valleys and plains. Villages grew into flourishing towns and some became handsome cities.

The Aryans brought their gods with them: Surya, the

God of the Sun, whose hair was flame, who drove forth in his chariot yoked to seven horses; Vayu, God of the Wind and Air, the very breath of man; Yama, who ruled the realm of the dead; Indra, Lord of Heaven, the giver of rain, a warrior god who rode a celestial elephant and brought victory to those whom he favored; Agni, God of Fire, the much-loved guest and friend of men, who dwelt on the hearth and who carried to all the gods, with his flames, the sacrifices offered to them.

These are only a few of many deities, for the Indians have a splendid imagination. As the Aryans came into India, they encountered other races, most of them less advanced than they were; as they penetrated southward, they met stronger tribes who fought against them. The invaders won, but they also adopted many of the beliefs and the deities of those whom they conquered.

Soon earth and sky, forests, rivers, and mountains, were filled with these airy creations. Many of them were kind and helpful to men; these were the gods and goddesses, "the shining ones"; but there were also demons, mischievous and murderous, who fought even against the gods and sometimes defeated them. Higher deities, too, appeared to prove that men were thinking beyond sun, and wind, and rain. These were great figures: Brahma, who created the universe; Vishnu, who preserves and guards it; and Shiva, who destroys. The last two were, and still are, the most important. Vishnu has saved the world from disasters that threatened it, and when mankind is in need, he is born as a man and by his teaching and example shows people the way out of trouble.

One of the earliest stories about him tells of a time when a powerful demon had defeated all the gods and had taken possession of the three worlds: the underworld, the earth, and the heavens above. Since the gods were powerless, Vishnu decided to outwit the tyrant. He was born as a

Vishnu. *(The Metropolitan Museum of Art, Mr. and Mrs. John D. Rockefeller Gift)*

dwarf to two saintly hermits who lived in the forest. He grew up there, waiting for his chance to save the universe. At last he heard that the demon was about to perform a great sacrifice, and that, as part of the ceremony, he must give generous alms to anyone who asked of him. The dwarf made himself look still meaner by dressing as a beggar, and appeared before the throne.

"O lord of the three worlds," he said, "will you give a poor beggar as much land as he can cover with three steps?" The demon laughed as he looked at the little creature. "As much as you can cover with three steps," he said, "you may have as your own." Then Vishnu took his own mighty form. He placed one foot upon the lower world, the other on the earth, and with the third stride he reached the heavens. So the world was saved.

Shiva is the destroyer, but he destroys only that everything may come to life again. For the Hindus believe, as modern scientists are also speculating, that the universe is evolved and then again dissolved, in vast cycles of time, like outbreathing and inbreathing.

> All beings, creator and worlds alike, return again and again. Those who know that the day of Brahma lasts for thousands of ages and that his night also lasts a thousand ages—they know the true meaning of day and night. When the day comes, all the visible creation arises from the invisible; and all creation disappears into the invisible when night comes.[1]

Indian mythology is rich and varied; there are countless delightful stories like that of Vishnu, and they are still important in the life of the people. But the Indians have always seen beyond their myths, for they have thought deeply, persistently, and thoroughly about the nature and the purpose of the universe and the mysteries of human life and death. In the very early days they perceived that behind the forces of nature, which had been deified as so many gods, there must be one power; that behind the multifarious appearances of the universe, there must be unity.

Before there was any recorded history, men left their homes and their occupations and went into the forests. The climate allowed them to live there in all seasons; they found enough fruits, berries, and edible roots to keep them alive. There, living in small huts thatched with leaves, they could give all their energies to concentrated thought. These are the sages, called *rishis,* who founded the basic religion of India. The thoughts of these great men form the scriptures, the holy books of Hinduism, which are called the Vedas. There are four of them, and each one is made up of three different parts: hymns to the gods; the rituals of worship; and philosophical discourses, called the Upanishads. The Vedas were composed before there was a written language and are believed to be inspired "by the very breath of God." Although there are many different sects in the Hindu religion, the Vedas are the foundation of them all. In addition there are many books containing laws and commentaries on the Vedas, which are also sacred, but not thought of as revealed by God.

One of the Vedic hymns declares: "In the beginning there was neither being nor not-being; there was no sky and no heaven above the sky. What power was there? What contained this teeming universe? Was it a fathomless abyss of waters? There was neither death nor immortality; there was neither day nor night. Only the One was breathing, self-contained, peaceful. Only the One existed; there was nothing else, above or beyond."[2]

"One only, without a second. . . . From this One

comes the whole of creation, breathed out, as it were, or as smoke comes from fire."

This One is Brahman, the Sanskrit name for God. It is not a person; It cannot be defined or perceived by any sense, yet It is everywhere present in Its creation. It is larger than large and smaller than small, "smaller than a mustard-seed, smaller than the kernel of a canary-seed," and It dwells in the heart of every creature. It is the soul of man, the Atman; therefore God is often called the Self, and the human personality, the self. "At whose behest does the mind think? Who bids the body live?" says one of the Upanishads. "Who makes the tongue speak? Who is that radiant being that directs the eye to form and color and the ear to sound? The Self is the ear of the ear, the mind of the mind, the eye of the eye. That which cannot be expressed in words but by which the tongue speaks—know that to be Brahman . . . That which cannot be understood by the mind but by which the mind understands—know that to be Brahman . . . That which is not seen by the eye, but by which the eye sees, know that to be Brahman . . . That which is not drawn by the breath, but by which the breath is drawn—know that to be Brahman. . . . Blessed is the man who while he yet lives realizes Brahman. The man who does not realize Him suffers his greatest loss. When they leave this life, the wise, who have realized Brahman as the Self in all beings, become immortal.

"It is to be found by undivided love; in It all beings dwell and by It was the universe stretched forth."[3]

Another Upanishad says: "In the heart of all things, of whatever there is in the universe, dwells the Lord. It alone is the reality. Wherefore, renouncing all vain appearances, rejoice in it! The Self is One. It is within all and It is without all. He who sees all beings in the Self, and the

Self in all beings, hates none. To the enlightened soul, the Self is all. For him who sees everywhere Oneness, how can there be delusion or grief?"[4]

This same truth is told over and over, in vivid and beautiful story, sometimes in dialogue, sometimes in splendid poetry.

In one of the Upanishads there is this story. When he was twelve years old, a boy was sent by his father to study the Vedas under a teacher. After twelve years he came home; he had learned the holy books by heart and was very proud of himself. His father said, "My son, you think yourself very learned and are very proud. Tell me, have you been taught to hear what cannot be heard, to see what cannot be seen, and to know what cannot be known?"

"What sort of teaching is that, sir?" asked his son.

"My dear, by knowing one clod of clay, you can know everything that is made of clay, for the difference is only in name and form, but the truth is that all are clay," answered his father. "By knowing one pair of scissors, you can know all that is made of iron, for the difference is only in name and form, but the truth is that all are iron. This is the teaching that I mean."

"Surely my venerable teachers did not know these things, or they would have taught them to me," said his son. "Please teach me yourself, sir."

"In the beginning there was One only, without a second," said the father. "It thought, 'May I be many; may I grow forth.' Thus out of Itself came the universe, and It entered into every creature. It is the subtle essence of all things. That is the truth; That is the Self. And you, my son—you are That."

"Please, sir, teach me more about this Self."

"Be it so. Bring me a fruit of that fig tree."

"Here it is, sir."

"Break it."

"It is broken, sir."

"What do you see there?"

"These tiny seeds, sir."

"Break one of them."

"It is broken, sir."

"What do you see there?"

"Nothing at all, sir."

"That subtle essence which you cannot see," said the father, "is the very life of the whole tree. In that subtle essence all things have their being. That is the truth; That is the Self. And you, my son—you are That."[5]

The highest purpose in life is to realize, not just to believe, that the spirit of man is one with God, to know the presence of God within one's own heart. This is bliss immeasurably greater than any other joy. But one must not only be pure in heart to know God; one must be able to quiet not only one's feelings but also one's thoughts in order to concentrate on that one purpose. This is far too difficult for most people even to try, and no one knew this better than those wise men who retired into the forest for that very purpose. Most people do not even want to think about such things; their prayers, then and now, are usually for wealth and happiness. It would take more than one lifetime to know God.

What, then, happens after this life is over? The Aryans, like most early peoples, could not believe that the parents, the grandparents, sometimes the children, whom they loved, were lost forever when they died. They believed that their ancestors lingered with them and watched over them; they, in return, made offerings of food and water to them and assured them that they were not forgotten. Indeed, it was believed that the spirits of their ancestors could not survive without the care of their descendants, and this is one reason why sons were desired, for daughters married and became a part of their husbands' households while the sons, from generation to generation, preserved the memory of their forebears.

As men thought more deeply, this belief gave way to the conviction that many lifetimes are needed before the heart can become pure enough to return to and be merged with God. They came to believe that we are born over and over again, with different bodies and personalities, until we finally are able to reach immortality. Each life is a lesson learned or an opportunity missed. For the Hindu believes, very literally, that as one sows, so shall he reap. If a person lives well, he is reborn in more favorable circumstances and, in his spiritual life, goes on from where he left off. If he lives badly, he is born in a difficult or degraded form and must work his way up again. This explains, they say, why some people are healthy, gifted, and rich while others are crippled, unhappy, and unfortunate. Each one is working out his *karma,* that is, the consequence of all his acts, good and bad, in every lifetime. No one can do this for him; no sacrifice offered by himself or anyone else can free him from the effects of his own deeds; he must work out his own salvation. This belief is known as reincarnation; that is, the soul is clothed, again and again, in a fleshly body.

Now all of this is very high doctrine, and those holy men, the rishis, knew that very few could understand the whole of it. They knew that most people need visible and tangible objects, or at least personal deities, to pray to and to adore. They did not deny the gods when they conceived a supreme, ineffable Spirit; the gods, they said, were manifestations of that Spirit, just as the rivers and mountains, sun and moon and living creatures, were. Those who understood this worshiped God in the images of the

Detail of the interior of a Hindu temple. *(Government of India Tourist Office)*

gods; those who could not understand continued to pray to Agni, to Surya, to Vishnu and Shiva, and to a multiplicity of other deities.

One of the great rishis was asked once by another wise man (for they loved to discuss these things), "Yagnavalkya, how many gods are there?"

"Three and three thousand, three and three hundred," answered the rishi.

"Yes," said the other, and asked again, "How many gods are there really, O Yagnavalkya?"

"Thirty-three," said the holy one.

"Yes," said his friend, and asked again, "How many gods are there really, O Yagnavalkya?"

"Three," he answered.

"Yes," said the other. "How many gods are there really, O Yagnavalkya?"

"One," said he.[6]

Now in addition to thinking out these profound questions, a society must also be built in which men can live safely and happily, for this, too, is an important part of any religion. As the population grew, small states were formed, each with its king. The ideal of kingship was a high one: the king was judged by the happiness of all his people. He must see to it that reservoirs were provided for the use of farmers and herdsmen, for there is a rainy season in India and then a dry one when stored water is needed. He must tax his people as bees take honey from flowers, without hurting them; he must encourage trade and industry, so that there would be no excuse for thievery and no one need lock a door. He must choose wise and honest ministers and have a holy man as his teacher and adviser.

Society was divided into four classes, or castes: first of

all, the Brahmins,* who alone had the right to be priests; the Kshatrias, who were rulers and warriors; the Vaisyas, who were farmers, tradesmen, and artisans; and the Shudras, who served the higher castes. These last were probably the native races whom the Aryans had conquered. The Sanskrit word for caste is *varna,* which means color, and the conquered people were darker-skinned than the Aryans. Besides, there was a sharp separation between them and the three upper classes: the Shudras were not allowed to study the Vedas or to take part in the religious ceremonies of the Aryans.

This social system was in the beginning a division of duties; each caste had its responsibilities and its privileges. But as time went on, people were restricted and often oppressed, for they could not escape from their caste and the occupation they were born to. In time, too, because of intermarriage and the increasing complication of society, many more castes were formed, even hundreds of them. And, since religion was so important, the Brahmins became very powerful. Only they could perform the public sacrifices which were often very elaborate and long; only they could teach the Vedas. They were the advisers of kings and were honored and supported by the other castes. At religious ceremonies riches were poured into their hands, and some of them became more tyrannical than any king.

There was one way of life in which there was no distinction of caste, except for the Shudra, to whom this way was not open. If a man left the world and all his possessions and went into the forest or wandered the

---

*Keep these words clear: Brahman = God, the supreme, ineffable Spirit; Brahma = a god, the creator of the universe; Brahmin = a member of the priestly caste.

streets as a beggar in search of God, nothing restrained him; and if he succeeded in his quest, he was honored above the Brahmins and above kings. It was said that if a man, or a woman, realized the Self within himself, his face shone with an inner light, and everyone knew what had happened to him and sought his teaching.

Ideally there were four stages, or steps, in a man's life. These applied particularly to Brahmins but also to anyone of the three upper castes, if he chose to take them. The first step was a time of study: a boy went to a teacher, a guru; sometimes he could stay at home, but usually he went to his teacher's house or to the forest if his guru were there. He served and obeyed this man, who was even more important in his life than his parents. When he had finished his studies, he came home, married, and became a householder. This was an important and honorable time, for society depended on the work of the householder, no matter what caste he belonged to. He pursued the three aims of worldly life: duty, wealth, and pleasure. However, when his sons were grown and his grandsons born, he was free to lay down all his duties as well as his possessions, and retire to the forest, to purify his heart and to find God. Many a powerful king, many a warrior or rich merchant, left everything and everyone he possessed and, clad in the simplest garments, became a forest-dweller. Often they lived in groups, gathered about some holy man; sometimes they lived alone, as hermits. Women, as well as men, could do this, either with their husbands or alone. In the Upanishads women sometimes took part in the endless discussions of doctrine and often asked keen questions and gave wise answers. If men or women chose to take this third step, their families understood what they were doing and did not stand in their way, for so it was ordained and the decision was honored.

There was still a fourth and final stage, if the spiritual

journey were to be complete. In this, one renounced everything except a ragged garment and a begging bowl. The sánnyásin,* as he was called, had not even a hut, but slept under a tree; he did not find and cook his own food, but accepted whatever was put in his begging bowl; he gave up his caste. He "saw himself in all creatures and all creatures in himself"; therefore he harmed no one, not even an insect, and feared no one; he possessed nothing and was at peace. His purpose was to be at one with God, and therefore not to be born again in the world but to be lost in the bliss of the godhead:

> He who even here, before the liberation from the body, is able to withstand the storms of desire and of wrath, he is the happy man. He who finds his joy within, his paradise within, his light within, that master of union is one with God. Those whose sins are worn away, who have cut the knot of separateness, who are self-mastered, who delight in the welfare of all beings—they become one with God.[7]

This has been the ideal structure of Indian society, right up to modern times.

Most people, of course, remained in the caste and condition they were born to; they did their work and sought wealth and pleasure. Only a few people follow the ultimate teaching of any religion. Many Hindus, however, went into the forests and a system of physical and mental discipline was worked out to help them in their purpose. It is called *yoga,* which means uniting; the English word *yoke* comes from the same root; one who practices it is a

---

*pronounced sán-yáh-sin

yogi, or *yogin.* It cannot be attained by any outer activity; it is an inner effort of the mind and spirit.

Since the purpose of yoga is to be at one with God, the yogi must first of all free his heart of anger and fear and desire, and of malice toward any living creature. Nonviolence, *ahimsa,* is of the first importance. At the same time he must control his thoughts, which must be turned inward and concentrated upon one sole purpose. The whole person, including the body, must be subservient to this end.

The mind is controlled through meditation. This is a word and a practice that is known both in the East and in the West; but while it is known to few Western people, it is familiar to every Hindu. The yogi sits, preferably cross-legged, with the back and neck erect but relaxed; his breathing is controlled and rhythmic. The beginner finds his mind filled with distracting thoughts and images which are hard to drive away. He is advised to fix his attention upon some aspect of God, or to repeat again and again a holy name, in order to shut out anything that can divert him. It may take years to achieve complete concentration; only the very gifted can speed the process. "When all the senses are stilled, when the mind is at rest, when the intellect wavers not, then, say the wise, is reached the highest state. This calm of the senses and the mind has been defined as yoga."[8]

There are several degrees of meditation. Many people who are not yogis practice it for an hour or two each day, in order to bring peace, or order, or love, into their daily activities. The yogis who practice it intensively tell us—and prove what they say—that there are faculties of the mind, and of the body, that most people do not know about simply because they do not find and use them. The highest form of meditation leads to the state of consciousness that the Hindus call *samadhi,* and that is known in the West as mystical experience or cosmic consciousness. It is that "immeasurable bliss" that is spoken of in the Upanishads, a recognized experience that cannot be disregarded in this age of science and skepticism.

Yoga was known to the earliest forest-dwellers, who taught it to their disciples. Those wise men knew that people have different natures and abilities, and they taught different yogas, so that each person could choose the one for which he was most fitted.

One yoga is the way of love, or devotion; it is usually directed to a personal manifestation of Brahman: a god, an incarnation such as Krishna or Rama, of whom you will hear later. This is bhakti yoga. The same discipline of mind and heart must be followed, but the intensity of love and longing, directed only toward the beloved being, can carry one to samadhi.

There is the yoga of work, or action, which can be practiced by any householder while living his daily life. It is known as karma yoga. Anyone who undertakes it offers all his acts and all his work to God, and cares nothing for the results or the rewards of his deeds. Some of the greatest karma yogins have been kings and warriors.

Jnana* yoga and raja yoga are both disciplines of the intellect and are very difficult, since realization must be reached by the intensity of thought alone.

The student of yoga must have a guru; besides the traditional wisdom and instruction that a teacher can impart, it is believed that invaluable help can be given through direct communication between him and his student. Also, the faculties that can be discovered and released through this discipline are powerful and, without

---

*pronounced jinyana

the guidance of the guru, can be misused and cause damage both to the student and to other people.

At this late date, yoga is attracting much attention in the West. Though few people go through with it to the end, they find that the easier stages keep the body and mind fit and alert.

Right behavior is the very foundation of any society. If men's desires and passions are not controlled, either from without or from within, there is no peace, no opportunity for the joys and labors that life offers. Religions try to control from within. Besides, there is in every people an intuitive belief that what men do has a direct relation with the way the universe around them moves and functions. Rules or ideals of behavior, usually called morals, have been taught by every religion, and the world would be a far happier place today if we had obeyed their teaching.

The moral standards of Hinduism are very high. They can be learned most pleasantly in the two great epic stories, the Ramáyana and the Máhabhárata. The Indian imagination operates here in all its magnificence; each of these epics is filled with dramatic and delightful incidents. The Máhabhárata, by far the longer of the two, also contains many complete tales, each one significant and many of them very beautiful. Though the epics were composed thousands of years ago, they are still a vital part of Indian life. They are told by parents to their children, by teachers to their students, by innumerable storytellers in villages and towns. They are danced and dramatized not only in India but in those places influenced by Indian culture: Indonesia and the countries of Southeast Asia. Their heroes and heroines are held up as examples to young and old alike.

The Ramáyana is the story of Rama, the eldest son of a wise and strong king who lived in northeastern India about 1500 B.C. Rama is believed to be an incarnation, an avatar, of Vishnu, who, in a lesser degree, was also incarnate in Rama's three younger brothers, Bhárata, and the twins, Lákshman and Shátrughna. They were Kshatrias, and were brought up as warriors and rulers. They learned to ride horses and elephants, to drive war chariots, and to use the bow, the mace, and the sword, especially the bow, which was the principal weapon in those days. Rama was the leader, the strongest and cleverest and best in everything; in archery he was the equal of the gods.

When their father was old, he decided to give the throne and the burden of government to Rama, who was his heir. Everyone was delighted, for they loved Rama above all men. But now evil enters the tale: the king had three wives, and each of his sons, excepting the twins, had a different mother, though they treated all three queens with equal respect and love. Bhárata's mother, influenced by a wicked serving-maid, demanded of the old king that he give the throne to her son and banish Rama to the forest for fourteen years. She had power over the king because he had once granted her two boons, which she had never claimed. Now she claimed them and would not change her mind. In spite of his grief and his pleading she persisted in her demand, and he had to keep his word, for it was unthinkable for a king to do otherwise.

The next morning, when Rama was to be crowned and all the city was rejoicing, he was summoned to the king's presence, where the queen told him what had happened, for his father could not speak for sorrow. Rama's face did not change; he obeyed at once, saying that of course his father's promise must be kept and that he would go to the forest that very day. His beautiful and beloved wife, Sita, went with him, as well as his brother Lákshman. The joy of the palace and of all the people was changed to despair as these three were driven from the city in the royal chariot. The old king died a few days later of his grief.

Now Bhárata was away, a week's journey, visiting his grandfather, when all this came about. He was sent for immediately, for he must perform his father's funeral rites and rule the kingdom. But Bhárata was made of the same stuff as his brother. He was furious when he heard what had happened; he reproached his mother bitterly and set out for the forest immediately to find Rama and to bring him back. He begged his brother to return and become king, but Rama refused. Their father's word must be kept, all the more since he was dead. When Bhárata saw that all his tears and his pleading were in vain, he took Rama's sandals and raised them to his head in sign of respect. "These," he said, "shall rule the kingdom until you return, and I shall be their humble minister."

Rama and Sita and his brother Lákshman loved their life in the forest. They built a hut on a lovely mountain-side, bathed in the river, found and cooked their food, and delighted in the forest creatures and in the beauty of each season. But Rama and Lákshman were warriors, protectors of men. The holy people of the woods came to them and told them that a band of demons was persecuting and killing them, and Rama promised his help. The demons attacked him, and he killed them all with his deadly arrows; but in so doing, he aroused the wrath of their powerful king, who lived in Ceylon. In revenge, this evil creature stole Sita away by trickery and carried her off to his splendid city. What could Rama and Lákshman do, who had not even a horse or chariot to ride, against the armed hordes of their enemy?

They made an alliance with the king of the monkeys,

who summoned all the monkeys in the world to make an army and to rescue Sita. At the head of this eager, rollicking host they marched to the southern tip of India, built a causeway across the ocean—parts of which you can now see—and, after a terrific battle, defeated the demons, slew the king, and freed Sita, who had nearly died of grief and terror. Then they came triumphantly home, for the fourteen years of exile were over, and Rama reigned long and gloriously, with his brothers as his ministers.

The virtues celebrated in this story, told so briefly here, are honor, truthfulness, faithfulness, disregard of power and possessions for their own sake, self-control, bravery, justice, compassion, and devoted love. Faithful and happy marriage is honored in Hindu legends and rarely found in those of other countries. Rama is worshiped to this day in India as the perfect son, brother, husband, warrior, and king; and Sita as the perfect woman, faithful, tender, and compassionate to all creatures, even to her tormentors when she was in captivity.

It is an old story, told and retold over many centuries. Probably its lovable characters were just human beings to start with; the demons may have been an alien people who had settled on Ceylon and were invading the southern part of India, and the monkeys a friendly, uncivilized tribe living in the woods. But it makes a far better story as it is told.

The other epic, the Máhabhárata, is a complicated and splendid tale, far too long to be told here, except for one incident. It is the story of a quarrel between cousins over the inheritance of a kingdom. On one side are five brothers, just and honorable, great warriors; on the other, their implacably jealous and spiteful cousin, backed by his family and his friends. In spite of all that the brothers can do to end the quarrel peaceably and justly, in spite of their forbearance under the plots and persecution of their cousin, it comes at last to a mighty battle between the two sides, each with its allies and their armies. After eighteen days of fighting, no warriors are left alive save the five brothers.

When the two armies, in all their splendor, are drawn up for battle, one of the brothers, Arjuna,* the greatest warrior of them all, is overcome with pity and horror for the bloodshed that he knows will follow. He will have to fight and kill men whom he loves and honors, members of his family, and his teacher. In this story, too, an avatar of Vishnu takes part. He is Krishna, a friend of the five brothers; he will not fight for them, but he consents to be Arjuna's charioteer. Arjuna tells him that he cannot fight; that he would rather die than kill those who are drawn up in battle against him. Krishna answers him, and the dialogue between them is one of the greatest spiritual poems in the world. It is called the Bhágavad Gita—for short, the Gita†—the Song of God, and it is as important as the Vedas in its religious teaching.

Krishna first speaks of death and immortality. "You grieve for those who need no grief," he tells Arjuna. "The wise do not mourn either for the dead or for the living. For there was never a time when I did not exist, nor you, nor any of these kings of men; nor shall we ever cease to be. . . . These perishable bodies belong to the eternal lord of the body, the imperishable and immortal spirit. . . . It is never born and never dies and will never cease to be; it is not slain when the body is slain. As a man puts off an old garment and takes a new one, so the spirit leaves its mortal body and enters a new one. Weapons cannot wound it, nor can fire burn it; waters do not wet it, nor can

*The accent is on the first syllable.

†The *g* is hard, as in get.

the dry winds parch. . . . This lord of the body dwells immortal in the body of each one; therefore do not grieve!"[9]

He tells Arjuna that he must fight this battle, which is a just one. He is a Kshatria; if he does not fight, he will fail both in duty and in honor. He would not have been born in that caste if he were not destined to do the work of a warrior and a ruler of men. But he must fight without hatred and without any desire for victory or reward; he must dedicate all that he does to God and remain firm and at peace within himself. Good and bad fortune, gain and loss, victory and defeat, must be the same to him. Only so can he engage in this terrible combat without sin.

"He who abandons an action, saying, 'It is painful,' does not know the truth," says Krishna, "but he who does the required work, saying, 'It ought to be done,' giving up passion and hatred and all desire for reward, his work is pure. With his doubts cut away, he accepts his work, whether it is painful or pleasant. . . . The four castes have their different duties, ordained by their natures. . . . Heroism, energy, firmness, prowess, refusal to flee in battle, generosity, and noble leadership are the duties of the Kshatria. A man reaches perfection by devotion to his own duty, when through his work he worships God, from whom all things come and who is all in all. . . . He should not abandon it because it is imperfect, for all action is clouded by imperfection, as fire is clouded by smoke. . . . He whose mind is unattached, who has conquered self, who is free of desire, will reach that perfect state which is beyond all action.

"The Lord, O Arjuna, dwells in the heart of every creature. Take refuge in Him with your whole heart and you shall find peace, the eternal resting place."[10]

The virtues set forth in this great poem, and in the whole epic are, again, honor, justice, forbearance, self-control, gentleness, patience, purity of heart, generosity, and compassion. In one part of the story the eldest of the brothers is tested by one of the gods in a series of riddles. The last question is: "What, O King, is true knowledge? What is ignorance? What is mercy and what is the highest duty?"

"True knowledge is to know God," answers the king. "Ignorance is not to know one's duty. Mercy is to wish happiness to everyone. The highest duty is not to harm any living creature." Though they are Kshatrias and bound to fight for justice, this was the ideal. In the end, when the brothers are old, they leave the kingdom to Arjuna's grandson, the only surviving heir, and become pilgrims.

When those great poets who wrote the epics said "any living creature," they did not mean only men. Animals, too, insects, any form of life was sacred, since it lived only because God was its life. The sages who dwelt in the forests ate only the fruits, the berries, and the plants that they found there, or sometimes raised little patches of grain. It is always said of them that the animals browsed unafraid around their dwellings and that tigers and poisonous snakes never harmed them. Rama and his brother sometimes hunted, though they and Sita lived most of the time as the hermits did. At the time of the epics many beasts and birds were sacrificed to the gods, but gradually these primitive customs decreased. The Hindus found that it was against their conscience to kill animals, and they became vegetarians. This concern for all living creatures is sometimes carried to extremes in India, which is a land of extremes. The cow has always been worshiped for her generosity in providing milk, butter, and curds, while her dung is used as fuel and is also mixed with the clay of peasants' huts. Shiva rode on his great white bull, Nandi, whose stone image often reclines on the porch of his master's temples. Cows and bulls are therefore never killed and are free to go where they will; they wander through the streets and the markets, and few people will drive them away. Monkeys are honored for their part in Rama's victory. Sita would never have been saved if the strongest and cleverest of them, Hánuman, had not leaped from the Indian shore over to Ceylon to find her. He has his own temples, and monkeys swarm over them and other shrines, where they are often charming and lovable, and often a nuisance as monkeys will be.

HINDUISM TODAY

These are the foundations of Hinduism—the Vedas, the laws and commentaries that underlie the high moral standards, and the two great epics, including the Bhágavad Gita. All of them were written long ago, as were all the scriptures of the world. How do they apply to modern times?

Hinduism is not organized as Western religions are. There is no church, no authority, except that of the scriptures and of any Brahmin who teaches them. For there is a priesthood but no hierarchy; no Brahmin is above any other, except in wisdom and spiritual experience. There is no congregation, no regular time of meeting; there are beautiful temples, large and small, but people go to them when they choose, make offerings to the gods, and say their prayers. There are wonderful festivals, almost one for every month, when crowds of people assemble at holy places, and traditional rituals are performed by the priests, but worship is mostly a private matter. Each house has its shrine, to whatever god the family chooses; each village has its deity, sometimes represented only by a stone, and it may be a very local deity, known only to that village. For this reason India is said to have millions of gods. The most important have always been Vishnu and Shiva, who are adored all over the country. These are towering figures, each with his own profound significance and symbolism. Vishnu reveals himself in such great avatars as Rama and Krishna; Shiva, who was once the destroyer, is also the creator, for Brahma has receded and become a rather shadowy figure.

The belief in evolution and involution is symbolized in the many sculptured figures of Shiva as the "lord of the dance." His dance provides the primal energy that brings the universe into being and then pervades it. His dancing also brings it to an end. His four arms represent his powers. The drum that is held in one of his right hands calls the world into being; the lifted right hand protects it; the fire in the left hand is the symbol of destruction. The foot on which he stands tramples upon evil; the lifted foot releases the soul from false belief; and the remaining left hand points downward to this release. Many interpretations have been given to this rhythmic figure, and Shiva as lord of the dance has been worshiped widely to the present day. A modern philosopher writes that the meaning of his dance is threefold: first, it is the source of all movement in the cosmos; secondly, it releases countless souls from the snare of illusion; lastly, it takes place within the human heart.

The female aspect of deity has always been recognized in India. It is expressed in the lesser deities, the gods, for in the idea of Brahman, of Absolute Existence, there is no thought of sex. The wife of Shiva is represented sometimes as Uma, the charming goddess of the Himalayas, where Shiva spends much of his time, and sometimes as Kali, who has two aspects. She is represented as a terrible figure who wears a necklace of skulls and brandishes a sword and a severed head, to whom animals are

The dance of Shiva. The god in this aspect is known as Nataraja, the lord of the dance. Bronze sculpture, about 1000 A.D. *(The Metropolitan Museum of Art, Harris Brisbane Dick Fund, 1964)*

still offered in sacrifice in spite of the reverence for all life that is such an important tenet of Hinduism; she is also adored as the Divine Mother, the female face of deity.

It must always be remembered that in such a vast country as India, where many races have mingled, there is every degree of belief. To many people the gods and their images are very real and meet their spiritual needs. Others look upon them as symbols or rejoice in their beauty as people in the West enjoy the religious arts of Europe. And many modern Hindus, like many people in other countries, do not believe in any God at all.

There have always been many different sects and many schools of philosophy, for everyone has always been free to think and to believe as he chooses. The most important of these schools is the Vedanta. The word means "the end of the Vedas"; that is, the Upanishads, which come at the end of the four sacred books. The faith of the Vedanta is based on the statements found there: that God is One and is to be found in the heart of all living creatures.

In spite of, or perhaps because of, the very looseness of its organization, its freedom of thought and worship, its tolerance of all other faiths, Hinduism has survived many dangers and calamities and is strong and vital today.

The history of India is a stormy one. The country was too large to be ruled by one central authority before the days of modern transportation. It was, therefore, most of the time divided into smaller kingdoms, and there was often war between them. Nevertheless, for two thousand years or more, India was in the hands of its own rulers, and it prospered. In the first four centuries A.D. all of its holy books were put into writing; philosophy and the arts flourished; the myths and stories, too, were written and put into durable form in splendid architecture and sculpture. During these centuries Indians traveled to the east: to the countries of Southeast Asia, to Ceylon and Indonesia, and established their culture there. Some of the most splendid Hindu architecture and sculpture is found in Cambodia and Indonesia; the epic stories are dramatized in puppet and shadow plays and are exquisitely danced there, to this day.

The greatest danger to India was invasion. Its rich river plains were very tempting to the nomadic peoples of central and western Asia, and it was conquered by the Turks in about A.D. 1000 and a few centuries later by the Mongols. Both Turks and Mongols were Muslims and brought the religion of Muhammad with them. In 1498 four Portuguese ships, led by Vasco da Gama, rounded the Cape of Good Hope and reached the west coast of India. Other Europeans followed, lured by the riches of the Orient, and seized upon ports and territory for trading purposes. The British prevailed over the French and the Portuguese and gradually took over more and more territory until by the middle of the eighteenth century they held the whole of India. They ruled over it for about two hundred years, until it regained its independence in 1947.

These conquests, the Turkish, the Mongol, and the British, brought two foreign and powerful religions into India: Islam and Christianity. During the centuries of Muslim rule, millions of Hindus were converted to Islam, some forced into it, some because it was profitable to adopt the religion of one's rulers, and some because in Islam there is no caste: "All Muslims are brothers." When India became independent in 1947, nearly a quarter of her population was Muslim, and the great country was divided into two states, India and Pakistan.

Many Christian missionaries came to India after the British conquest, and their religion was a challenge to Hinduism, although relatively few Indians were converted. Christianity lays great stress on loving and serving one's "neighbor," that is, anyone who is in need, and the educated and intelligent Indians became aware of things in their society that needed change and reform. Many of the missionaries, as well as British officials, were scholars; they learned Sanskrit and became deeply interested in the Hindu scriptures. They translated the Vedas and the Bhágavad Gita, which were widely read in Europe and America. In their enthusiasm they found beautiful Sanskrit literature that had been forgotten or neglected by the Indians themselves. That great Hindu, Mahatma Gandhi, first read the Gita in English in London. Western knowledge and scientific achievement were brought to India; educated Indians spoke English and often other European languages, and the intellectual interchange was profoundly valuable.

Whether this interchange caused it or not, there was a great revival of Hinduism during the nineteenth century, and it is still going on in the twentieth. The admiration of foreigners aroused the pride of Indians in their great literature and tradition. The introduction of printing brought the sacred books to many more people. Religious societies were formed, strongly influenced by Christianity, led by high-caste, intellectual Hindus. They were opposed to the worship of gods and images, interested in the basic truths of all religions, and devoted to the reform of social conditions. They returned to the profound doctrines of the Vedanta, based on the Upanishads.

We are not concerned in this brief account with history, economics, or politics, except as they are affected by religion; but in India everything is affected by religion. The revival of Hinduism and its effects on the life and history of the country can best be understood through the lives of three or four men who embodied this renewal of spiritual strength.

RAMAKRISHNA PARAMAHAMSA

In 1836 there was born in a village of Bengal a boy who became known as Ramakrishna, to which was added later the title *Paramahamsa,* given only to people who have become great saints. His parents were Brahmins; they were poor but always generous to anyone who needed help, and they were very devout.

From the first he was an unusual boy, merry and active and affectionate. When he was six or seven years old, walking home from school one day, he saw a dark thundercloud spreading over the sky. Suddenly a flight of snow-white cranes passed across it, and the boy was so entranced by this beauty that he fell senseless on the path and was carried home by some neighbors who found him there. He did not care much for school and enjoyed far more the company of storytellers and wandering monks who repeated the incidents of the epic stories and other poems and songs about gods and heroes. These were often dramatized in his village, and he took part in the plays.

When he was eighteen, his older brother became a priest in the temple of Kali, the Mother Goddess, at Dákshinéswar, near Calcutta. It was a magnificent temple, surrounded by gardens, on the banks of the sacred Ganges River. It was built by a woman of the Shudra caste who also endowed it with enough money for its maintenance. She had to present it, however, to a Brahmin, for no priest would officiate in a temple belonging to a woman of her caste. Ramakrishna went with his brother and helped him in his duties; when his brother died only a year later, the young man of nineteen took his place. There were other shrines in the great temple, and other priests lived there.

Though he performed his duties, he had only one

desire and one purpose, and that was to realize the presence of God, as the scriptures had taught him to do. His first experience of that blissful state was through the sculptured image of Kali, the wife of Shiva, in whom he saw the Divine Mother, the tender and compassionate aspect of God. His way at this time was the yoga of love—bhakti yoga. "Men weep rivers of tears because a son is not born to them," he said, "or because they cannot get rich. How many are there who weep in sorrow because they have not seen God? He who seeks Him finds Him; he who with intense longing weeps for God has found God." He always defended the worship of images, knowing that it was a step to higher realization. "If a man thinks of the images of gods as symbols of the divine, he reaches divinity. It is God who has provided so many forms of worship. The mother prepares different kinds of food for her children, to suit different stomachs."[11]

He, too, was to go further than his devotion to Kali. Up to this time he had been without a guru, for he had been able to undertake hard spiritual discipline by himself. Now teachers came to him. The first was a woman, a *sánnyásini,* as women are called who have taken the last step in the pilgrimage of life. She taught him that all the pleasures of the senses, however small and innocent, must be given up if one is to attain the highest goal, and she gave him rigorous training in yoga.

His most important teacher was a wandering monk who passed by one day and saw Ramakrishna sitting in front of the temple. He recognized the young priest at once as a fellow seeker and stayed at the temple to teach him. Under his tutelage Ramakrishna became a sánnyásin; he gave up his caste and its distinguishing marks, and all possessions, and put on the loincloth and the brownish-yellow robe that set him apart as a man whose only purpose was to find God. His guru taught him the Vedanta faith: that there is but One, One without a second; that he must go beyond his devotion to Kali, who is "God with form" to "God without form." This was very hard for Ramakrishna, but his teacher forced him to do it, and he very quickly attained the highest degree of samadhi, where he felt himself at one with the unmanifest, impersonal Brahman. "In so short a time," his guru said of him, "he has done what it took me forty years to do." "How does one feel in samadhi?" someone asked him in later years. "As a fish feels," he answered, "when it is put back in the water, after being kept on land for some time."

He was twenty-eight years old at this turning point in his life. During all the years of his searching, some people had thought him slightly mad. He would go for days without food or sleep and fall into deep meditation no matter where or with whom he happened to be. A devoted nephew took care of him. But now people understood what had happened to him and came to learn from him. The brilliant men who had started the religious societies came and learned anew the values of their own faith for he was a living example of its teaching. All sorts of people came to ask questions and to listen to him. Like all spiritual teachers he spoke simply, often in parables. He was as simple and direct as a child but saw through any insincerity or ostentation. He wrote nothing, but his disciples took down much of what he said and made a book of his sayings.

He believed, as all Hindus do, that all religions, if faithfully followed, lead to the same end. But a spoken truth was never enough for him; he always wanted to realize it, to prove it through his own experience. A devout Muslim came to live in the temple compound of Dákshinéswar; Ramakrishna learned from him the doctrine and practices of the teaching of Muhammad. He said the Muslim prayers, wore Muslim clothes, and ate Muslim food; he studied the doctrine and concentrated his thought upon it, and in a few days he found the same spiritual experience that he had gained through his own faith. Later on, he studied Christianity with the same intensity and came to the same conclusion. He loved to talk with anyone, of any sect or belief, who truly believed and lived what he professed, and always advised them to follow the way that they had been taught. "There are many ways that lead to the temple of Kali," he said, "and many that lead to the house of the Lord. Each religion is one of those ways."

Toward the end of his life a group of young men gathered about him and became his disciples. After his death in 1886 they formed an order of monks named after him. There were about a dozen of them at first; one by one they left their homes and their studies and became sánnyásins, devoting themselves to the intense spiritual discipline that their master had taught them. They were not wanderers, begging their food; they lived together in a house that was given to them by an admirer of Ramakrishna, and this house became the first monastery of the order. They gave a new direction to the holy life, for these young men came from educated families and were convinced, as were many Hindus of their time, that their country was in need of social change and reform.

They went out into the world to help the poor and the needy. Many people joined them, and new centers were formed. They opened schools and colleges, agricultural and industrial schools, hospitals, homes, libraries, open to everyone regardless of caste. They have done splendid relief work in times of famine or other calamities. There are now more than sixty monasteries and as many missions of the Ramakrishna Order.

One of the brothers, the Swami* Vivekananda, is widely known in the West as well as in India. He was especially loved by Ramakrishna and was the leader of the first group of young disciples, when they founded the order. Later, in 1893, he went to America when a Parliament of Religions was held at the Chicago World's Fair. The enormous audience was amazed by his fine presence, his powerful speech, and his presentation of Hinduism, which few people knew anything about. He lectured far and wide, talked with scholars and churchmen, and established the Vedanta Societies which still flourish here. He also went to Europe where he made the same impression and established Vedanta Societies in several countries.

MAHATMA GANDHI

The most famous of the men who exemplified in their lives the teachings of Hinduism is Gandhi, who was also given a title of sainthood. He is known as *Mahatma,* which means literally "great soul." He is the only man who has brought his religion to bear directly and uncompromisingly upon the political, economic, and international affairs of the modern world.

He was born in 1869 into a subdivision of the Vaisya caste, that of tradesmen and farmers, but his father and grandfather were prime ministers in some of the small princely states in the west of India. He was well educated; he learned both Sanskrit and English in school, and later he spent three years in England studying law. There he found the Bhágavad Gita, which was to become his lifelong guide and comfort, "his mother" as he called that great poem. He also read the New Testament and was impressed particularly by the Sermon on the Mount,

*Swami means a holy man or religious teacher.

which, of course, he found very similar to the Gita in its teaching.

When he was twenty-three, a business firm of Indian Muslims sent him to South Africa to settle a lawsuit there. A great many Indian workmen had gone to South Africa as indentured laborers; that is, they were bound to work for a certain number of years for whoever hired them, no matter how they were treated. There were also Indians of other occupations, some of them prosperous merchants, living in South Africa, which at that time was a British colony.

Gandhi found out, during his first day in that country, that Indians had a hard time there. They were "colored"; they could not travel first class on the railways or stay in hotels; there was a curfew—they must be in their houses after 9:00 P.M. Worse things followed. Indians were not allowed to vote even though they were citizens of the country. All marriages except Christian ones were invalid; this meant that no Indian wife was a legal wife and that the children were illegitimate and had no legal rights. Worst of all, it was decreed that when an indentured laborer's term of service was over, he must pay each year a tax of three pounds (fifteen dollars at that time and far more than fifteen dollars of our present money) for himself, his wife, and any grown child. With the pay that he received, this was impossible; the law was meant to drive the laborers back into indenture, which was little better than slavery.

Gandhi went to South Africa, intending to stay for a year to settle a lawsuit. He stayed for twenty years, and before he left every one of those unjust laws had been repealed because of him.

It is the way in which he did it that concerns us. In the world's eyes he was powerless—a young insignificant-looking man, with no money, no influence, no army or police behind him. He was a Hindu: he believed that God dwelt in every heart, and since God is truth, all men will respond to truth if they perceive it. He was unable to hate or to strike another person, but he believed that the power of the spirit was stronger than any other power, and he proved what he believed. The scriptures taught him that, in order to use, or to be used by, the power of truth everything else must be given up; all sense of "I" or "mine" must be abandoned before God could work through one. He had much to give up: he had been married at thirteen to a girl of the same age; he had two sons when he came to South Africa, and two more were born there; he made a very good income with his law practice; and he was a person of intense and warm feeling. He did not renounce all these ties at once; year after year, through meditation and reading and prayer, he gave up one thing after another, trying, as he said, "to reduce myself to zero." In doing this, he became one of the most dynamic personalities of his time.

He set himself to right the wrongs that Indians suffered, pledging himself to two principles: truth and nonviolence. He used every means except violence; he wrote innumerable pamphlets, articles, and letters for African and Indian papers; he started a newspaper called "Indian Opinion"; he formed an association of Indians of all faiths in South Africa. He was always courteous and friendly to his opponents; he told them what he intended to do before he did it and asked them to repeal the laws that he was fighting. English men and women joined him and worked with him all his life. When the Boer War came, although he sympathized with the Boers, he organized an ambulance unit that did fine work; when the plague broke out in Johannesburg, he worked among the sick and dying. He was a tireless worker; besides all his writing, correspondence, and organizing, he worked physically, nursing the sick, cleaning latrines, washing clothes, for he had a passion for cleanliness. He did first whatever he asked other people to do.

With these methods, Gandhi fought the three-pound tax. When all appeals failed, he led the indentured miners of Newcastle on strike. He told them that they might be beaten, perhaps killed, surely jailed, and that they must accept everything and never commit any act of violence. He himself had already been beaten, kicked, knocked down, and imprisoned; he accepted it without resentment. All the miners, five or six thousand people, obeyed him, and they were all thrown into prison, together with Gandhi, his wife, and other women who worked with him.

This aroused a storm of indignation in India and England and South Africa. Thousands of indentured laborers, other than miners, joined the strike. The government found itself in danger of having to imprison fifty or sixty thousand people, which would be difficult and embarrassing. It gave in; the tax was rescinded. Later, by the same means, the marriage laws were changed. The vote had already been granted, and other restrictions eased. The power of truth—*sátyagráha,* as it is called in India—had won.

When Gandhi returned to India in 1915, he was ready to give his life for the welfare of his country. With the consent of his wife, he had pledged himself to chastity, poverty, and service; he became the perfect karma yogin, the Gita in his hand. He believed, as Ramakrishna did, that all religions were true but none truer than his own; he did not have to look beyond it for his inspiration. The Indian people, steeped in their faith, recognized his sainthood, or spiritual power, immediately. He was amazed to find enormous crowds waiting to greet him, raising a shout that soon became familiar, *"Mahatma Gandhi ki jai!"* (Victory to Mahatma Gandhi!) And Mahatma he remained, although he vastly preferred the title of brother, which he had won in South Africa, or, in his later years, that of *Bapu,* or father. To it was usually added the suffix *ji* which denotes respect and affection: Bapuji, Gandhiji, Mahatmaji.

Already in South Africa he had formed a community of his family and others who worked with him; they had lived on the land and raised their food, just as the sages in the early days had lived in the forest surrounded by their disciples and students. Such a community is called an ashram; his friends came to India with him, and they founded an ashram near the city of Ahmedabad in western India.

The caste system, over the centuries, had become very complicated; there were hundreds of castes and subdivisions of castes, all separate, in small ways, from one another. There were also several million people who were below all caste. They were outcasts and were known as untouchables because their touch, or even their shadow, was considered defiling. They could not enter a temple or use a village well; no caste Hindu would accept anything from their hand; even one of the lowest caste would not eat with them. They lived apart and performed the meanest and most unpleasant tasks. Gandhi considered their condition one of the first things that must be changed in India; it was a shame and a disgrace.

Soon after his ashram had been established, a family of untouchables came there and asked to join him; they were educated people, the man a teacher. Gandhi and his community accepted them at once, for one of his purposes was to do away with the unbearable condition of these people. He gave them a new name: *Harijans,* or children of God. A storm of protest arose in the neighborhood; the merchants threatened to cut off their supplies, and rich men in the city who supported the ashram withdrew their funds. Gandhi decided that the only thing for him and his companions to do was to go and live in the untouchables' quarter of the city and earn their living there, which would make them untouchables, too. While they were planning this, a rich Muslim came to the ashram and gave them enough money to support it for a year.

Ever since Gandhi had begun his dedicated life, he had set aside a time, in the early morning and in the late afternoon, for prayer and meditation. No matter how busy he was—and he was sometimes so busy that he had only two or three hours' sleep—no matter where he was, he always observed these times. He was rarely alone; in the ashram all his companions met together. They chanted verses of the Gita and prayers; they sang hymns; often he spoke to them, and often they sat in silent meditation. There were two Christian hymns that he loved: "Lead, Kindly Light" and "Abide with Me." When he traveled, hundreds of people gathered around him, morning and evening, for these prayer meetings.

Before he returned to India, he had worn European clothes; now he adopted the peasant's dress: a white cotton cloth wound round the waist and thighs, drawn up between the legs and tucked in at the waist. In hot weather he wore only this; when he traveled or in cooler weather, he wrapped himself in a voluminous shawl of white wool or cotton. He went barefoot or wore sandals of wood or leather. The cloth that he wore was spun and woven by hand; for one of his principal concerns was the revival of the village handicrafts, which had suffered badly from competition with the machine-made goods brought in by the British and forced upon the people.

Anyone who had a grievance came to him: sharecropping farmers, factory workers, peasants unjustly taxed. He

Mahatma Gandhi. *(Henri Cartier-Bresson: Magnum Photos Inc.)*

So long as man clamors for the I and the Mine,
His works are as nothing;
When all love for the I and the Mine is dead,
Then the work of the Lord is done.

—Kabir

always told them the same thing: to strike peacefully, without hatred, and to suffer patiently whatever was done to them. He led them himself if he could, and the difficulties were justly settled. He soon became known all over India, and both the Indian and the British leaders knew that nothing could be done without this small, indomitable man.

Gandhi had at first been willing for India to be a part of the British Empire, but self-governing. He admired the British and had many friends among them. Soon, however, he was convinced that complete independence was necessary. The story of the winning of India's freedom is a long and exciting one, too long to be told here. Many brilliant and devoted men and women worked untiringly for their country's welfare, as Gandhi did. He was their spiritual leader, their guru, their father; the one on whom everyone depended and could trust. One or two episodes may throw light on his leadership.

When he first declared for independence, he urged everyone to practice noncooperation: that is, to boycott foreign cloth and other products that could be made in India; to refuse to work for the British government or to attend British schools and colleges. When this seemed too slow a method, he advocated civil disobedience, which meant the breaking of laws that were considered unjust. He opened this campaign in a spectacular way.

The manufacture and sale of salt were government monopolies, and there was a tax on the sale. This bore most heavily on the poorest people, who must buy salt and had so little money. Gandhi tried, as he always did, to have the laws changed, but with no result. Then, with about eighty companions, he walked from the ashram to the seacoast, more than two hundred miles away. By the time he arrived, several thousand people had joined him, and the whole country was watching to see what he would do. On the beach he picked up a handful of salt left by the tide. It was a symbolic act, and it set off a wave of civil disobedience throughout the country. Salt was made in every way known to man, sold freely, and given away. Gandhi was put in prison, and so were tens of thousands of other Indians, among them many prominent men and women. But the salt monopoly and the tax were given up.

This was done with no violence at all; people submitted peacefully to arrest. But during the long struggle for independence, violence sometimes broke out, and men were killed on both sides. When this happened, Gandhi immediately called off any activity that was going on against the government. He blamed those who had lost control of themselves, but he blamed himself most, for it was he who had taught them both resistance and nonviolence. On such occasions he fasted: he ate no food for a given time, sometimes for three days or a week, once for three weeks. He did not consider this a punishment but a purification, to make himself a better instrument for God. All his life he had believed in fasting as a purifier of body and spirit. He also knew that it was a weapon, for it usually brought people to his feet in a few days.

His most crucial fast was in 1932, when the British, under all this pressure, were giving the Indians a greater share in the government. The Muslims and the untouchables were both minority groups. The British offered to set aside for them certain seats in the legislative assemblies, to give them better representation. But in order to fill these seats, Muslims could vote only for Muslim candidates and untouchables only for untouchables. Some of the leaders of both groups were pleased with this arrangement; but Gandhi saw that it emphasized the separation of these groups from the great Hindu majority. He wanted only complete equality and unity among all Indians of whatever faith or caste. He tried his strongest persuasion; when that failed he wrote to the British prime minister: "I have to resist your decision with my life. The only way I can do it is by declaring a perpetual fast unto death."

He was in jail at the time, as many others were. He did not take the fast as well as he had taken former ones; after only a day or two, he became very weak; after three or four, his doctors feared for his life. The whole country was in a turmoil; men worked desperately to come to an agreement that they, as well as he, could accept. The British were nearly as worried as the Indians. They opened the prison gates to anyone who wished to consult him; they brought his wife and his devoted secretary from other jails to be with him. On the fifth day of the fast the Indian parties came to an agreement; they took it to Gandhi, and he murmured his assent. It was cabled to London on a Sunday, when the ministers were away. They hurried back, studied the document until midnight, and cabled their agreement. Meanwhile Gandhi, barely able to speak, lay on a cot in a prison courtyard; no one could have appeared more powerless. On Monday morning the new pact was announced, and that afternoon he broke his fast with a glass of orange juice.

In 1947 India became free, with the friendliest feelings on both sides. The last viceroy was cheered enthusiastically as he drove through the crowded, bedecked streets. But Gandhi took no part in the festivities. On August 15, Independence Day, he sat alone, spinning and fasting. For in one respect he had failed, and the failure broke his heart and brought about his death. India was divided; Pakistan and East Pakistan (now Bangladesh) formed a separate

Muslim state. He had worked all his life for unity between the two faiths, and after the partition he worked to stop the terrible violence that followed it.

On January 30, 1948, as he walked to the afternoon prayer meeting that he never missed—this time in a friend's garden in Delhi—he was assassinated by a young man who belonged to a fanatical anti-Muslim party.

VÍNOBA BHAVE[12]

One of Gandhi's disciples carries on his work for the poor peasants in the same extraordinary way that he had done, by sátyagráha, the power of truth, and ahimsa, nonviolence.

His name is Vínoba Bhave,* and he is working now in India to get land for landless farmers. Farming is difficult there: the rich river plains are exhausted by thousands of years of ignorant cultivation; they are also overpopulated. Worst of all, the peasant rarely owns any land; after several conquests it is in the hands of landlords, and a peasant who cannot pay his rent can be evicted, or else he falls into the hands of the moneylender, who charges such high interest that the debt can rarely be repaid. Although much land has been redistributed, this is still true in many parts of India.

Vínoba, as he is usually called, comes of a well-to-do Brahmin family and is well educated. He went through school and college and read widely but his one desire was to be a sánnyásin and to give his life to serve his people. He took the vow of chastity and poverty when he was twelve years old, and he never broke it. He left college in a western town and went halfway across India to the holy

*pronounced Bah-vay

city of Benares, on the Ganges, where he hoped to study Sanskrit and to find out what was going on in his country. Soon after he arrived he heard Gandhi speak at the University of Benares, and Vínoba knew at once that he had found his guru. He was twenty years old, and Gandhi was more than twice his age. He joined the ashram, and when he came to it, Gandhi said to his companions, "Here is one who has come to give as well as to receive, to teach as well as to learn." The Mahatma adopted the young man as his spiritual son.

Vínoba was sent to form an ashram of his own, where he and other devoted men and women worked with the peasants, starting small industries—weaving, sandal- and shoe-making, potteries, dairies, and so forth. It was after Gandhi's death that he started his crusade to get land for the peasants.

His method is simple. He walks through the country, stopping in every village on his way, asking landlords to give him one sixth of their land to distribute among those who have none. And it is usually given to him—as simply as that. He himself possesses nothing; he dresses as Gandhi did in a dhoti, or loincloth, a shawl, and sandals. When he arrives in a village, people assemble from the surrounding country, sometimes hundreds, sometimes thousands. He holds a prayer meeting in the open air, then asks for land. "If you had five sons," he says, "you would divide the land among them. Think of me as your sixth son and give me my share." He chose the number five in memory of the five brothers, the heroes of the Máhabhárata.

In the very first village that he went to, forty Harijan (untouchable) families came to him and said that they favored communism because the communists were offering to give them land. "Let us see," said Vínoba, "what your own village can do for you." That evening he held his meeting, surrounded by a great crowd of people. He told them about the forty families. Then a landlord stood up. "Sir," he said, "I will give them a hundred acres." Generosity responded to generosity; the Harijans said that eighty acres, two apiece for each family, would be enough because they would farm it together. Perhaps someone else could use the other twenty.

The news spread like wildfire. Everywhere crowds met him and land was given. In one village he met no response; the chief landlord made many excuses; not a hand was raised when Vínoba made his appeal. "It does not matter," he said. "I shall go to the next village, and God will move the hearts of others." Then a Harijan came forward, dressed in a worn, much-washed loincloth. "I have a quarter of an acre," he said, "but I do not need it, for I work in a tanning factory and earn enough to support my family. I will give it." "God has answered my prayers," said Vínoba. "Now I know that there are many more who are ready to give." A hundred hands went up, and there was a burst of applause; the landlord who made so many excuses gave a fifth of his 850 acres. The quarter acre was accepted from the Harijan, and then given back to him.

In a year Vínoba walked nearly four thousand miles, at a rate of about twelve miles every day, and at the end owned 170,000 acres of land. Every acre was deeded to him; in every village committees were formed to distribute the land, and followers of his (they, too, came by the hundreds) stayed behind to help and to keep the accounts. Gifts came in from people who never saw him; those who had no land gave other things—oxen and wagons, plows, bricks, tools, and seeds. A maharaja gave 100,000 acres. Another, not to be outdone, gave 100,001. In three years over 3,000,000 acres had been given and distributed to the peasants. Religion is full of paradoxes: only a man who possessed nothing and desired nothing could call forth such giving. Only one who had "reduced himself to zero" could have had the power to bring about a peaceful revolution of this magnitude.

Vínoba's life and work appealed, as Gandhi's did, to the whole country, and innumerable people offered their land and themselves to him. Hundreds of men and women, many of them distinguished leaders in government and education, either followed him or went out themselves to gather in more land. One new gift particularly pleased him: a whole village gave up its land and owned and worked it communally. This was a return to the old self-sufficient community that had originally existed in India. Within a year of this first gift of a village, more than four thousand others had pooled their land. Vínoba's followers did not leave these villages when the land was given, for they knew that the peasants would need help in cultivating it properly and in establishing the industries that would make it prosperous. Some always stayed to help them.

One incident that occurred during Vínoba's long pilgrimage cannot be omitted. In northern India, not far from the important cities of Agra and Cawnpore, is the dangerous valley of the Chambal river, which falls into the Jumna. There are wild, steep ravines along this river which for centuries have been the strongholds of bandits and guerrillas known as dacoits, whom no government had yet been able to drive out. They lived by robbery and murder, and the people of the surrounding country were in constant danger.

Vínoba, always on foot, had been to Kashmir and to the Punjab. On his way back, he went into the Chambal valley because a dacoit chief, in prison and awaiting the death sentence, had written to him, asking to see him. People crowded to him there, as they did everywhere, telling him their troubles, the deaths of sons and brothers killed by the bandits. He talked to them about love and self-restraint and fearlessness, saying that good as well as evil were in all men's hearts; that the possession of wealth created robbers and that generosity would change them. To everyone's amazement, the dacoits, first one or two, then ten or twelve, came to him and surrendered. "Baba [grandfather]," they said, "we have done wrong. We won't do it any longer." At his evening prayer meeting one day, twenty of them laid their rifles and their cartridge belts at his feet.

They knew that they would go to prison for their past misdeeds. Vínoba promised them justice and that their families would be taken care of during their absence. The police left them with him for four days and then took them to jail. In India there is a festival when sisters tie a sacred thread around the wrists of their brothers and give them sweetmeats in token of affection. When the dacoits went off to jail, the girls in Vínoba's company and in the town bound the threads around the prisoners' wrists, and Vínoba blessed them. He left a group of his workers there to look after the prisoners and their families. Gandhi's and Vínoba's work is still going on.

These men—Ramakrishna, Gandhi, Vínoba—and other men and women, too, are the saints of Hinduism, for saints are only people who obey to the utmost the teachings of their faith, whatever it may be. Only a profound and vital religion can produce such people, and they, in turn, keep it alive.

O Servant, where do you seek Me?
Lo, I am beside you.
I am neither in temple nor in mosque;
Neither am I in rites and ceremonies,
Nor in yoga and renunciation.
If you are a true seeker, you shall at once
see Me;
You will meet Me in a moment of time.

Kabir says: "O Sadhu! God is the breath
of all breath."

—*Kabir*

Stone head of the Buddha, from Siam. *(Courtesy, Museum of Fine Arts, Boston)*

PART THREE

Buddhism

To commit no evil,
To do all that is good,
To keep one's thought pure:
This is the teaching of all the Buddhas.

Buddhism is an outgrowth of Hinduism, a branch of the great tree of Indian religion and philosophy. Its truths, its moral code, and its methods are based on the long tradition of Hinduism, for the Buddha, who founded it, was born a Hindu. There are important differences, however, which have led to its being called a separate religion. Buddhism does not accept the Vedas as its authority and therefore cannot correctly be called a Hindu faith. The Buddha denied the existence of Brahman, or God, and also of the human self, or ego; as he saw it, the universe was governed by law alone. This was contrary to the teaching of the Vedas, and yet he promised the same bliss that the Upanishads declare as the supreme attainment of human life.

His doctrine was a clarified, systematized, new interpretation of the Indian thirst for the infinite; for in his time

Hinduism had become confused with many theories and many sects; it was also overlaid with ritual and was too dependent on the priesthood. Buddhism does not recognize caste or the power of the Brahmins; anyone who is qualified may preach its doctrine. It rejects sacrifices and acts of worship, and lays all its emphasis on the effort and conduct of the individual.

This new, strong faith was founded nearly twenty-five hundred years ago, long before the time of Gandhi and Vínoba.

The Buddha means "the enlightened one"; it is not a name but a title that is given to men of great wisdom. The man who is most widely known by that title is the founder of Buddhism, the religion that is named after him.

He was born in the northeastern part of India, which at that time included a part of what is now Nepal; it is close to the splendor of the Himalaya Mountains. His father was the ruler of one of the small states into which northern India was divided. His family name was Gótama; his given name, Siddhartha,* which means "he who has reached his goal." He was born about 560 B.C., during that extraordinary time when an upsurge of thought and aspiration passed through the civilized parts of the world.

There is no written account of his life, though writing was widely used in his day. But the main facts, and incidents told by the Buddha himself, were remembered by his followers and handed down from one to another for centuries before they were finally written. Many legends were also told about him during those centuries. The resultant story is partly fact and partly legend, and both reveal the great spiritual teacher and the love and reverence in which he was held.

---

*See pronunciation chart, page vii.

Gótama Siddhartha was born, then, in the country of the Sakyas, the son of its ruler, the rajah. His mother died when he was a week old, and he was lovingly cared for by her sister, who was also the rajah's second wife. At the time of his birth a very wise man was at his father's court and was asked to look upon the child. "You have begotten a wonderful son," said the sage. "If he remains within the home, he will become a mighty ruler over the whole earth; but if he leaves the home for the homeless life, he will become a savior of mankind." His father was troubled by this prophecy, for he wanted his son to succeed him and to become a great king. Therefore, the story goes, he surrounded the boy with every pleasure and never let him see anything ugly or painful that might disturb him and arouse questions in his mind.

Once, when Siddhartha was a young boy, he went out with his father who, following the custom of those times, was plowing with his own hand the first furrow of the season. Siddhartha sat down in the shade of a rose-apple tree and before long fell into a deep and serene meditation. His father did not see him there and returned to his palace, but later he missed the boy and sent a servant to find him. He was still sitting under the tree, lost in meditation, and although hours had passed and sunlight and shadow had changed, the shade of the tree had not moved but still sheltered him.

In time, he married a lovely girl and had a son; but still the rajah tried to keep him within the palace and its pleasure grounds, lest he awake to the truths of life. One day Siddhartha told his father that he wished to drive out and see the world. The rajah ordered the streets to be decorated and cleared of all dirt, and sick or old people to stay within doors. The young prince rode out in his chariot and looked at the fair city and the smiling people. As he was returning, a very old man who had not heard the rajah's order came, bent and hobbling, down the street. "What has happened to that man that he looks so weak and miserable?" asked the prince. "He is old, my lord," answered the charioteer, "as we shall all be some day, if we do not die before our time."

Siddhartha's heart was shaken, partly by pity and partly by disgust, and he ordered the charioteer to drive him home. His wife asked what was troubling him, and he told her what he had seen. "How can anyone rejoice in youth and beauty if that is the end for us all?" he asked.

He drove out again and yet again. He met a sick man, groaning with pain, and the charioteer told him that any man may suffer such pain and illness. He met a funeral procession; he saw the stiff, cold body being carried to the funeral pyre, and the weeping family following it. This time the charioteer's answer was firm. "Whatever is born must die," he said. "To this we must all come, my lord."

Lastly they met a sánnyásin, clad in a yellow robe, carrying a begging bowl; his face was calm and radiant. Siddhartha stopped the chariot and asked the man why he had become a sánnyásin. "I wished to conquer my self and to win peace and freedom from all ills," answered the man, smiling.

That night Siddhartha rose from his bed and dressed himself. He went softly to his wife's room, where she lay with their little son by her side. He would have liked to caress her and the baby once more but feared to waken her. There had been feasting and music in the palace that evening, and in its hall the dancing girls lay asleep with their instruments beside them. He walked quietly past them and left the palace. He wakened his charioteer and told him to saddle his favorite horse, Kánthaka. As he was being saddled, Kánthaka thought, "My girth is being drawn much tighter than when I am saddled for a ride in the park. My master must be going forth this night into homelessness," and in his delight he neighed loudly. The gods, however, were watching this momentous departure, for they wanted Siddhartha to achieve his purpose. A Buddha was a far higher being than a god and they, too, would need his help. So they muffled with their hands the sound of Kánthaka's neighing and held up his hoofs lest they strike too sharp a sound from the stones of the courtyard and waken sleepers in the palace. Quietly the prince went out with his faithful servant and rode on all through the night, until at dawn they found themselves beside a river.

There Siddhartha dismounted, and laid off his robes except for a single garment; he took out his sword and cut off his long hair. The robes and sword, the locks he had cut off, he gave to the charioteer, saying to him, "Take these to my father and tell him that I have gone forth into the homeless life."

When Kánthaka had to turn back without his master, his great heart broke and he died. The charioteer, who before had only one sorrow, the loss of his master, now had two and went back, weeping, to the city.

When he found himself alone, Gótama, as he was called henceforth by his companions, did what any Hindu would do who sought the truth: he looked for a teacher. He had heard of two who were famous for their wisdom, and he went first to one and then to the other and learned all they had to teach. But he was not satisfied; he wanted to know why men suffered and how they could be freed from suffering, and his teachers could not tell him. So he joined a group of five hermits who lived in the forest and were seeking enlightenment in the time-honored way by fasting and by severe discipline of body and mind. Gótama outdid them all and for six years disciplined himself in the most rigorous ways. At last he was living on only one sesame seed a day; his body was shrunken almost to a skeleton; his skin was black and shriveled. One day as he was returning from a bath in the river, he fainted from weakness.

When he came to, he realized that his mind was not being purified, but rather weakened, by this terrible training. He remembered the serene and blissful meditation he had attained as he sat under the rose-apple tree when he was a happy, healthy boy. A girl passed by and saw him sitting there, weak and emaciated; she brought him a bowl of rice cooked in milk, and he took it gratefully and ate it. After that he ate, frugally but normally, and felt his mind refreshed and strengthened. But his five companions thought him a backslider and left him.

Shortly afterward he felt strong enough to find for himself the truth that he sought. He sat down, cross-legged, under a fig tree and vowed that he would not rise until he had accomplished his purpose. Concentrating all his power of mind and spirit on that one goal, he passed from one state of meditation into another until at last he reached, in the highest degree, the state of consciousness that is called nirvana. There he found all his questions answered. "And thus perceiving, thus beholding," he said later, "my mind was freed from desire, from the craving for life, from delusion. And this knowledge came to me: rebirth is ended, the holy life fulfilled; what was to do is done; this world is no more for me."

He was tempted to stay in the bliss of this experience; to remain forever in nirvana and to let his body fall to the earth and die. For he thought, "The truth, which is sublime and peace-giving, is difficult to understand. It will remain hidden from those who love the world. If I preach it and men do not understand, it will bring me only weariness and loss." But Brahma the creator, so they say, appeared before him and, after greeting him respectfully, said, "Alas, the world will perish if the Blessed One does not teach the Law. There are many whose minds are barely covered by the dust of the world; if they do not hear the truth, they will be lost. Be merciful to them!"And Gótama looked with his enlightened perception at the world and saw that there were indeed many who were able to understand. So he decided to teach them the truths that he had found and to end their searching.

Some say that he remained for seven days under the fig tree, which, after that, was called the Bodhi, or the Bo tree, the tree of wisdom. During that time he thought out the details of his belief and of the doctrine that he was to preach all the rest of his life. Some say that he stayed there for seven times seven days. When all was clear in his mind, he thought, "To whom shall I first teach this doctrine?" He thought of the five companions who had left him and knew that they had gone to the Deer Park in the holy city of Benares. So he went there on foot in his hermit's robe, gathering his food each day in his beggar's bowl from willing villagers.

When he reached the Deer Park, his former companions saw him approaching. "Here comes Gótama," said one to another. "Let us not rise to greet him or show him any respect, for he has forsaken the holy life." Yet when they perceived the majesty and radiance of his presence, they rose to greet him and brought water to wash his feet. "How is it with you, friend Gótama?" one of them asked. "Do not call the Tathágata* by his name or address him as friend," answered Gótama, who knew very well what had happened to him. "For he has become the Buddha, the enlightened one. Listen to me, and I will teach you the Dharma, the Law, by which you, too, may attain the highest goal of the holy life."

---

*Tat-háh-ga-ta means "He who has thus come." The Buddha often referred to himself by that title.

The present temple at Buddgaya. This is the place where the Buddha attained enlightenment. *(United Nations)*

First he told them that he had not given up his former rigorous life out of weakness. He had found out that it was wrong either to indulge the body or to torture it with fasting and too rigorous discipline. One should live simply, eat what was put into the begging bowl, and clothe one's body in the yellow robes of the sánnyásin.

Then he told them, briefly and clearly, the truth that had come to him in his enlightenment. He had first sought it out of pity for the suffering of humanity, and his whole purpose was to free people from the pain and misery that he had seen. Therefore he said to them:

The First Noble Truth is the existence of suffering. Birth is painful, and death is painful; disease and old age are painful. Not having what we desire is painful, and having what we do not desire is also painful.

The Second Noble Truth is the cause of suffering. It is the craving desire for the pleasures of the senses, that seeks satisfaction now here, now there; the craving for happiness and prosperity in this life and in future lives.

The Third Noble Truth is the ending of suffering. To be free of suffering one must give up, get rid of, extinguish this very craving, so that no passion and no desire remain.

The Fourth Noble Truth is the Eightfold Path that leads to the ending of all pain. The first step on that path is Right Views: You must accept the Four Noble Truths and the Eightfold Path.

The second step is Right Resolve: You must renounce the pleasures of the senses; you must harbor no ill will toward anyone and harm no living creature.

The third step is Right Speech: Do not lie; do not slander or abuse anyone. Do not indulge in idle talk.

The fourth is Right Behavior: Do not destroy any living creature; take only what is given to you; do not commit any unlawful sexual act.

The fifth is Right Occupation: You must earn your livelihood in a way that will harm no one.

The sixth is Right Effort: You must resolve and strive heroically to prevent any evil qualities from arising in you and to abandon any evil qualities that you may possess. Strive to acquire good qualities and encourage those you do possess to grow, increase, and be perfected.

> The seventh is Right Contemplation: Be observant, strenuous, alert, contemplative, free of desire and of sorrow.
>
> The eighth is Right Meditation: When you have abandoned all sensuous pleasures, all evil qualities, both joy and sorrow, you must then enter the four degrees of meditation, which are produced by concentration.
>
> This is the Eightfold Path to the ending of all suffering.

When he had finished speaking, he asked his five listeners, "Have you thoroughly understood, O wanderers?" And one of them answered, "I have thoroughly understood, Lord." He became the first disciple and the other four soon followed him. The Buddha stayed with them in a hermitage near Benares and began to teach all who would listen to him. In a few months he had sixty disciples, and he sent them out to wander through the villages and towns, preaching his gospel. "Go forth now," he said, "for the benefit of many, for the welfare of mankind, out of compassion for the world. Proclaim the life of holiness; many will understand and accept it."

The Buddha's teaching was very clear and assured and systematic; he listed and numbered the points he wished to emphasize, beginning with the Four Noble Truths and the Eightfold Path; this made them easy to remember and follow. Many people turned to him because of the power of his personality and the clarity of his doctrine. His teaching freed them from dependence on the Brahmins and on the gods: sacrifices, supplications, and prayers did not matter. Salvation was in one's own hands.

The way out of suffering and out of continuous rebirth and death was not hard to understand; the Eightfold Path could be followed by anyone who wished to do so. The Buddha's philosophical teaching was more difficult but was eagerly welcomed by many of the brilliant minds that loved to debate and search out the problems of spiritual life. He taught that the whole perceptible universe, including its creatures, has no permanent being; that it changes at every moment and is in a state, not of being, but of becoming. Everything, therefore, being impermanent, is subject to growth and decay, to birth and death, to pain and sorrow. The individual self is also impermanent; it is a combination of different qualities, some inherited and some acquired, bound together, as it were, by karma, the sum of its own actions and thoughts, which leads it through lifetime after lifetime and death after death. This, indeed, is the crux of his teaching: it is the ego, the belief in self, that suffers, because of its separateness, its desires, its cleaving to and grasping of things and people, its clinging to life. "Whatever you cling to will fail you," he said. These desires send it spinning on the wheel of continuous births and deaths, which can bring only continued and repeated suffering.

The first step on the way to freedom is to realize that the self has no reality; after that it is not hard to shed the desires that the self clings to. As there is no self, so also there is no higher Self; the Buddha acknowledged no God, no Brahman, and therefore no indwelling spirit.

He did not deny all individual consciousness, for he said that during the first watch of the night of his enlightenment he saw all his past births. "And I called to mind my various fortunes in other lives: first one life, then two lives, then three . . . up to many thousand lives. Then I recalled the periods of many a world-arising and many a world-destruction. There was I. That was my name. To that family I belonged. That was my occupation." He was asked once what it was that went from one life to another, from death to rebirth. Was it not the same self? "If you light one lamp from the flame of another lamp, is it the same flame?" he asked. The questioner was puzzled; it was the same and yet not the same. "So it is with what passes from life to life," said the Buddha. It was the ego, the personality, that many of us love so dearly, that he denied.

In exchange for the belief in self and the consequent suffering, the Buddha offered peace and joy and, as soon as one was able to follow the Eightfold Path all the way, absorption into nirvana. Nirvana means "blowing out," "extinguishing," and most people believe that the Buddha meant it (as other Hindus did) to be the extinguishing of the passions of desire, anger, and sloth. But some people, both Buddhists and foreign scholars, have taken it to mean the extinguishing of life itself, the annihilation of all consciousness. So the controversy has gone on, from that day to this, as to what nirvana means, and the student must judge for himself. The Buddha would never say anything about it or even state firmly that a man continued to exist after his last death; he said that such talk was not profitable and did not help people to live the holy life. Nevertheless, he said once to his disciples, "Some hermits and Brahmins say that I am a destroyer, that I preach the extinction of being itself. But they accuse me falsely of the very thing I do not say. For I preach only suffering and the ending of suffering."

He spoke of nirvana as a reality beyond all sorrow and change, "unfading, still, undecaying, taintless, peaceful and blissful. It is the shelter, the refuge, and the goal." He often called it "the other shore." It seems unlikely that a man whose whole motivation was pity for mankind and a desire to put an end to their pain should offer at the end only eternal death. He also spoke of the attainment of it as "the full awakening." Does one awake to extinction?

One of his own followers came to him once and complained that he would not tell them whether the world is finite or infinite or what happens to the holy man who has lived his last life on earth.

"Did I ever say to you," asked the Buddha, "that I would tell you those things?"

"No, Reverend Sir," answered the other.

"You are like a man wounded with a poisoned arrow who, when his friends and kinsmen bring a physician, says to them, 'I will not have this arrow taken out until I know the caste of the man who wounded me, and his name, and the clan to which he belongs, and whether he was tall or short.' The questions that you ask have little to do with the holy life. Whether the world is eternal or not, birth, death, old age, sorrow, misery, and despair remain, and I can tell you how they may be extinguished," said the Master.

There seems to be no doubt that nirvana is the name for that same experience that lies at the end of all high spiritual endeavor, that the Hindus call "immeasurable bliss," that Ramakrishna found through following the paths of Christianity and Islam as well as the path of Hinduism.

The Buddha also taught many things that would now be included in the realm of psychology. One of the great discoveries of his night of enlightenment was that everything that we experience is caused by something that precedes it. He started with ignorance as the primary cause of all human woes. He was too wise to say that he knew the origin of life or of the universe, and he had no use for speculation. Starting with ignorance, he perceived a twelvefold chain of causation which leads to hatred, delusion, and desire, to death and rebirth. Deliverance comes with the realization that whatever begins must end and that whatever is caused can be stopped by removing the cause, which lies within oneself. It is said that two learned Brahmins were converted by hearing one of the Buddha's disciples recite this simple verse:

The Buddha has the causes told
Of all things springing from a cause
And also how they cease to be:
This does the Blessed One proclaim.[1]

These and many more profound and subtle questions of philosophy and psychology the Buddha discussed with his disciples, with learned Brahmins and scholars, and with anyone else who questioned him. They are just as interesting today as they were in his time. They are hard to understand and hard to practice, as he realized on the morning of his great awakening; but they are lightened and softened by the kindness and compassion that had made him decide not to pass forever into nirvana but to remain in the world to teach. To simple people he spoke simply and gently, often through poetic metaphors and parables.

Only a few people, ever, are ready to give up the world and to seek the truth of the spirit. Few, even of his own disciples, would reach nirvana; but anyone—a peasant, a shopkeeper, a warrior, or a king—could live the holy life wherever he was and whatever he was doing. That life is one of goodness, selflessness, purity, kindness to all creatures—animals as well as men—and steadfast spiritual purpose. Anyone, no matter how humble or how busy in the affairs of the world, who lived the holy life, was honored as a true disciple of the Buddha. He always emphasized one's own actions and one's own experience, drawing people away from the idea that a sacrifice or an act of worship would help them.

"All that we are is the result of what we have thought; it is founded on our thoughts, it is made up of our thoughts. If a man speaks or acts with an evil thought, pain follows him, as the wheel follows the foot of the ox that draws the cart. If a man speaks or acts with a pure thought, happiness follows him, like his own shadow, wherever he goes.

"By oneself the evil is done, by oneself one suffers; by oneself the evil is left undone, by oneself one is purified. Purity and impurity belong to oneself; no one can purify another.

"Not in the sky, not in the midst of the sea, not if one enters into the clefts of the mountains is there a spot in the whole world where a man may be freed from an evil deed.

"Although one man conquers a thousand times a thousand men, if another conquers himself, this man is the greater conqueror.

"He who, seeking his own happiness, injures or kills other beings who long for happiness, will not find what he seeks.

"Hatred does not cease by hatred; hatred ceases by love. This is the eternal law."[2]

"Yes, even if highway robbers with a two-handed saw should take and dismember you limb from limb, if your mind was darkened thereby you would not be obeying my teaching. Even then you must school yourselves thus: 'Our minds shall remain unsullied and no evil word shall escape our lips. We shall fill those robbers with a stream of loving thought, and forth from them it shall unfold and penetrate the whole world with constant thoughts of loving kindness, ample, expanding, measureless, free from enmity and all ill will.' Call to mind again and again this parable of the saw; it will make for your happiness and well-being."[3]

"As a mother cherishes her son, her only son, even at the risk of her own life, so must your love encompass every living creature. Cultivate towards the whole world . . . a heart of love unstinted, unmixed with a sense of differing or opposing interests. This state of heart is the best in the world."[4]

The Buddha was thirty-five years old when he sat under the Bo tree and became enlightened; he lived to be eighty. During the forty-five intervening years he spent his days teaching and preaching to all who would listen. He walked from village to village, from town to town, usually with some of his disciples; they took the food that was given to them and slept where lodging was offered. Peasants in the villages and rich men in the towns often vied with one another in offering hospitality, for holiness and learning were always honored in India. Towns and cities built halls and houses or set aside pleasant parks where these wanderers could stay and where learned men could meet and debate with one another. In such houses the Buddha and his followers would spend the late summer season when the downfall of rain made traveling impossible. There the people crowded to hear him, to bring him their problems and doubts, and there Brahmins, statesmen, and other sánnyásins came to question him. He received them all with serenity and kindness and perfect assurance, and he usually convinced them.

Not long after he began his ministry, he received a message from his father, asking him to visit his family once more. Though he was more than a hundred miles away, he undertook the long journey, on foot, with a few of his followers. With his shorn head and ragged robe, carrying his begging bowl, he appeared at the palace and was greeted with reverence by his father, as any holy man would be received, and by the aunt who had brought him

Stone sculpture of the Buddha teaching. From Borobudur, in Java. *(Rijksmuseum voor Volkenkunde, Leiden)*

up, who was also his father's second wife. These parents, his own wife and young son, he met again, and to them he was still the beloved son and husband, the unknown father; but to him they were as anyone else, neither dearer nor less dear, for he was free of all human affections and did not think of himself as the same person who had lived for nearly thirty years in his father's palace.

He did not live there when he went back; he and his followers stayed in a nearby grove of trees, as they loved to do. Early on the morning after they arrived, they went into the city with their begging bowls to receive their morning meal. Someone ran breathless to the palace and told the rajah that his son was begging in the streets. He found the Buddha and reproached him: "Come into the palace and eat with us," he said. "You are disgracing your family, my son. You are a Kshatria; no Kshatria begs for his food."

"I am of the lineage of the Buddhas," was the reply. "We always beg for our food."

Later, when he came into the palace courtyard, his wife said to her son, who was still a boy, "That glorious man in the hermit's robe is your father. Go to him and ask him for your inheritance; I hear that he has four great treasures." So the boy, Ráhula, went to his father and said to him, "Father, give me my inheritance." "I have no gold nor silver," answered the Buddha, "but if you are willing to receive spiritual treasures and are strong enough to bear and to keep them, I will give you those." "I am willing," said Ráhula and he followed his father from that time on. When the Buddha saw how grieved his own father was to lose his grandson as well as his son, he promised that he would never again take anyone who was under age into the order without the parents' consent. His half brother, Ananda, his aunt's son, went with him, too, and became his most devoted disciple, staying close to him all his life and taking personal care of him.

The Buddha founded an order of monks. This was a comparatively new thing in India, though there were many groups of men, professing different beliefs, who wandered about begging their food. But, like everything that the Buddha did or thought, the brotherhood he founded was systematic and carefully ordered, and it exists to this day in thousands of monasteries throughout Asia. At first it was very simple. The monks were homeless; they must not marry but be perfectly chaste; they ate their only solid meal before midday; in the evening they might eat lightly of fruit or juice. Their only vow was: "I take refuge in the Buddha; I take refuge in the Dharma [the Law, or doctrine]; I take refuge in the Sangha [the brotherhood]." Most of the time they traveled on foot about the country, preaching and teaching. During the rainy season they lived in the places given to them by the cities or by rich men and spent their time in meditation, in discussion of the doctrine, and in listening, first to the Buddha, then, as their number increased, to the wisest of the monks. In time, they were offered permanent houses and these were the first monasteries.

The monks and their master traveled about the northeastern part of India, from his birthplace in Nepal through the present state of Bihar, which takes its name from *vihara,* meaning monastery. They stayed often in Benares and in the city of Rajagriha, which has disappeared now but was once the capital of a strong kingdom. There was a mountain near it called the Vulture's Peak where they often retired for meditation and discussion.

Women often asked the Buddha if they might join his order, but he refused them. His wife begged that she might follow him, but he never allowed her to do so. His aunt, the mother of Ananda, was the most insistent. One time when the Buddha was staying in a banyan grove near his father's city, she came to him and begged him three times to allow her to leave her home for the homeless life, and three times he refused her. He left and went to another city, still in his father's territory but many miles away. Then his aunt cut off her hair and put on yellow garments and followed him on foot, with several other women. She stood in the porch of the hall where he was lodging, "sorrowful, sad and tearful, with swollen feet, and covered with dust." Her son, Ananda, saw her standing there and asked her why she had come.

"Because, alas, O Ananda, the Blessed One does not permit women to retire from household life to the homeless one, under the doctrine and discipline of the Tathágata."

"Wait but a moment," answered her son. "I will beseech the Blessed One to permit you to do so."

He told the Buddha that his aunt stood, weeping and footsore, in the porch, begging to be admitted to the order. Three times he asked his master to admit her, and three times he was refused. But Ananda was as persistent as his mother and tried another way.

"Are women able to attain to the holy life, to free themselves from rebirth, and to attain to sainthood, O Exalted One?" he asked.

"Yes, they are able," answered the Buddha.

"Then, if they are able to live the holy life, consider, sir, what a service this woman has already done for the world. As foster mother and nurse, she suckled the Blessed One after his mother's death. For her sake, pray let women enter the homeless life under the doctrine and discipline of the Tathágata."

His master relented and told Ananda that she might

join the order if she would accept the difficult rules that must not be broken as long as life shall last. He added one which made nuns always subservient to the monks; although they lived separately, the nuns must never stay in a place where there were no monks. He did not trust women very far.

Ananda brought the good news to his mother and asked her if she would accept the rules, which he repeated to her. "Just as a young woman, beautiful and fond of ornament," she answered, "would take a wreath of flowers and set it on her head, so do I take up these weighty rules that must not be broken as long as life shall last."

Joyfully she and the women who had come with her took up the holy life. Many more joined them, and some of them became both wise and saintly. The monks came to learn from them, and so did learned men from the cities where the nuns lodged.

The Buddha continued his ministry without any change in his way of living until he was eighty years old, a greater age then than it is now. Just before the time of his death he was living on the Vulture's Peak, near the city of Rajagriha. The king, whose capital city it was, planned to attack a neighboring clan, the Vajjians, and to destroy them; but since the Buddha was so near he thought it wise to consult him. So he sent a Brahmin, with great ceremony, to the Vulture's Peak to deliver the king's message. The Buddha did not answer but said to Ananda, who was standing behind him, "Do the Vajjians foregather often in public meetings, Ananda?"

"I have heard so, Lord," answered Ananda.

"So long as they gather often in public meetings in concord, and carry out their undertakings in concord; so long as they honor their elders and listen to their words;

so long as they revere their shrines in town and country and continue the proper offering and rites and protect and support the holy ones who live among them; so long, Ananda, the Vajjians will prosper and be strong. I taught them these things, and so long as they preserve them they will prosper."

The Brahmin understood. "So, Gótama," he said, "the Vajjians will not be overcome in battle." He took the message back to the king, and the Vajjians were left in peace.

The Buddha went on from place to place with a great company of disciples, and he taught them how to live together in harmony, for he knew that he would soon leave them. Everywhere they were received with honor, and people vied with one another to give them their noonday meal. At Vesali the Buddha was taken ill and was in great pain, but he overcame the illness, for he was not yet ready to leave his disciples.

They had been walking northward and were now in his family's territory, north of the Gogra River. He led them to the town of Kusinágara, to a grove of trees where there was a shelter for monks and travelers. "Spread me a couch between those two trees," he said to Ananda. "I am weary and would lie down." Ananda folded a robe, and the Exalted One lay down upon it, on his right side, as lions do, one foot resting on the other. "I am now grown old," he said, "my life is nearing its end. Just as a worn-out cart must be carefully tied together to make it move along, so, Ananda, the body of the Tathágata must be patched up to keep it going. Only when the Tathágata is rapt in contemplation and concerned with no external thing is his body at ease."

Then Ananda went to the door of the shelter and leaned against it and wept, thinking to himself, "Alas, I am but a student, and the Master is about to pass away from me, he who is so kind." The Buddha missed him and sent for him and when he had come, said lovingly to him, "Enough, Ananda! Do not weep! Have I not told you that it is in the nature of things that we must leave all that is near and dear to us? Whatever is born and brought into being must dissolve and die. For a long time you have been very near to me by acts and thoughts of love that are beyond all measure. You have done well, Ananda. Be earnest in effort, and you, too, shall soon be free!" And he praised Ananda to all the rest.

Then he sent him into the city to tell the citizens that the Tathágata would enter nirvana in the last watch of the night, for he knew that they would want to see him while he yet lived. Men and their wives, young men and maidens, gathered together and went to the grove and bowed down to the feet of their Master and then sat around him through the night, grieving sorely in their hearts and thinking, "Too soon the Exalted One will die! Too soon will the Eye of the World vanish away!"

The Buddha spoke to his monks: "It may be that some of you will think 'The word of the Master is ended; we have no teacher any more.' But you should not think that. Let the Truth and the rules of the order which I have laid down for you be your teacher after I am gone. And now, O monks, I take my leave of you. All the world is transient and subject to suffering. Work out your own salvation with diligence."

These were his last words. In the last watch of the night, passing through the ascending stages of meditation, he entered nirvana.

BUDDHIST TALES

In the forty-five years of his teaching, many, many of the Buddha's sermons, lessons, and talks were memorized by his followers and written down much later. They begin, "Thus have I heard," and end, "So spake the Blessed One." They make beautiful reading and are as valuable now as they ever were. Many stories inevitably grew about his memory. Some of them throw light on the Buddhists' attitude to the gods, whom they do not deny and whom the Buddha himself often mentioned.

Thus have I heard. At one time when the Blessed One was staying in a pavilion in the east grove, Indra, king of the gods, came to him, greeted him respectfully, and asked, "Can you state briefly, Lord, how a monk is wholly purified, perfected, made secure, and come to complete deliverance?"

"Suppose, O king of the gods," answered the Master, "that a monk understands that whatever he clings to will fail him. Understanding that, he penetrates the nature of all things and finds them impermanent and painful. Therefore he clings to nothing in the world and, unclinging, does not fear or tremble. Unfearing and untrembling, he attains his own deliverance and knows 'rebirth is ended, the holy life fulfilled; all that was to do is done; for me this world is no more.' So, stated briefly, O king of the gods, is a monk wholly purified, perfected, made secure, and come to complete deliverance."

Indra was pleased and satisfied with these words; he made obeisance to the Buddha and vanished from sight.

Now all this time that wise disciple, Shariputra, was seated nearby and heard all that was said. He thought to himself, "Is that great god really satisfied by the words of the Blessed One? Suppose I find out!" In a moment, by the spiritual power he had attained, he left the pavilion of the east grove and appeared in the heaven of Indra. The king of the gods was in his lotus garden, waited upon by the divine musicians and damsels. He welcomed Shariputra gladly, giving him an honorable seat and taking a lower one himself. The monk asked him whether he had been satisfied by the Master's words, and Indra said that he had understood them perfectly and had laid them to heart. Indeed, he repeated word for word what the Blessed One had told him.

Then he said, "There was once a great war, O venerable one, between the gods and demons, in which the demons were overthrown. I built a magnificent palace to celebrate that victory. Would you like to see it?"

Shariputra agreed, and Indra, with his chief ministers and many attendants, showed him all over the shining palace, saying constantly, "Look at this splendor, O venerable one; just look at that!"

The monk admired everything politely but thought to himself, "How foolish this god is, to value all this! Shall I give him a fright?" He put out his foot, and with his big toe he set the whole airy palace to shaking and trembling, till Indra and his ministers and all the celestial company were amazed at his magic power and their hair stood on end. Then, well pleased with his errand, Shariputra disappeared from among the gods and returned to the pavilion in the east grove.

One of Indra's ministers asked him, "Was that the Blessed One, the Master, who was just here among us?" "No," answered Indra, "it was one of his disciples." "You were fortunate to be visited by a disciple of such spiritual power," said the other, and added fearfully, "What if the Blessed One himself were to appear among us?"

After the Buddha's death, the fertile imagination of India fashioned many a story, especially about all the former lives that he must have lived in order to attain finally to perfection. With their strong belief in evolution, the Indians thought that each individual had come through innumerable experiences, starting at the lowest form of consciousness. They loved to tell of the time when the Buddha was born as an ox, as a dog, as an elephant, or as a quail. There is always some noble or wise act done by the bird or the animal who was to become the Buddha. Most of these stories are folktales of which the Buddha is made the hero; they make a charming collection and usually start, "Once upon a time when Brahmadatta reigned in Benares . . ."

So, once upon a time when that legendary king was reigning in Benares, the future Buddha was born as a hare who lived in a wood with three friends, a monkey, an otter, and a jackal. The hare always taught the others, telling them that alms must be given, the holy days kept, and the moral law always obeyed. One day, looking at the sky and observing the moon, he said to his companions, "Tomorrow is a fast day when alms must be given. Let us prepare food so that we may feed any beggar or holy man who may come to us."

They all agreed, and next morning each one went his way to find food. The otter brought back seven fishes, the jackal stole a lizard and a pot of curd from a peasant's hut, and the monkey gathered a bunch of mangoes. But the hare thought, "No beggar eats grass, which is my food, and I have no grain to offer him. If any beggar comes, I shall have to offer him my own flesh to eat." This virtuous thought struck up like a ray of light to the throne of Indra, who discovered whence it came and decided to put the hare to the test. He took the form of a Brahmin and stood by the four friends' dwelling and asked them for food.

The monkey, the otter, and the jackal all offered the food they had collected, but the Brahmin refused it for one reason or another. Then he came to the hare, and the hare said joyfully, "I will grant you a boon that I have never offered before. But I shall not make you break the moral law by taking a life. Go, friend, and make a fire and I shall leap into it, and when my body is roasted you shall eat it."

So Indra made a hot fire, and the hare approached it, first shaking his body lest any insects perish with him. Then he sprang up and, like a swan alighting on a bed of lotuses, he fell upon the flames. But the fire did not even singe his hair, and he said to the Brahmin, "Your fire is icy cold. What is the meaning of this, O Brahmin?" "I am no Brahmin," answered the god. "I am Indra and have come to test your virtue. O wise hare, this act of yours shall be remembered to the end of the world." Then he drew with his hand the figure of the hare on the orb of the moon and there it remains to this day.

Once upon a time when Brahmadatta reigned in Benares, the Buddha was born as a monkey. He grew up to be strong and wise and became the king of all the monkeys round about. He took them to a safe place, high in the mountains by the River Ganges. There was a beautiful mango tree growing beside the river; it bore delicious and fragrant fruit, and the monkeys swarmed about it when the fruit was ripe. The king saw that one great branch hung over the river, and he ordered the others not to leave one mango on that branch; indeed, he told them to pick the very flowers off, lest any fruit drop into the river and be carried away. "One day danger will come to us from the fruit falling into the river." he said.

And so it happened, for one day a hidden mango dropped off and was carried downstream and caught in a fisherman's net near the city of Benares. It was so large and perfect that the man took it to his king. The king ordered his boats out and sailed upstream with a great retinue of courtiers and archers. After many days they came upon the tree, tasted the mangoes, and set up their camp under the thick branches, as night was coming on.

At dawn the king was wakened by a great noise in the

tree, and looking up, he saw hundreds of monkeys swarming through the branches and eating the fruit. He called to his archers, "Surround the tree and shoot these thieves; let not one escape. We shall eat our mangoes with their roasted flesh." And the monkeys found themselves facing a hundred lifted bows on three sides and the river on the fourth.

Now the monkey king saw that the branch that had dropped its fatal fruit reached far out across the river and almost touched the branch of a tree on the opposite bank. He climbed swiftly up, flung himself out from the tip of the branch, which he held tight with his feet, and just caught the tip of the other branch with his hands. So he lay across the river like a bridge. "Pass quickly over me," he cried to the others, "and you will be safe." One after another, they took the road across his body, treading as lightly as they could and saluting and thanking him. But there was one who was jealous of him and saw this chance to be rid of him and to take his place. So he waited till the last, and when he crossed, he jumped on his chief's back and broke it, while he himself scampered off in safety.

The monkey king, helpless and in great pain, fell into the river. But the ruler of Benares had been watching all that went on with wonder and admiration. He ordered his boatmen to save the monkey, to lift him very gently and bring him to land. He clothed the wounded one in a yellow silken robe, laid him on his own bed, and fed him with comforting food and drink. Then he himself took a lower seat and asked the monkey to teach him how to be a king.

When the monkey died, the king had his body burned with as much ceremony as if he had been a ruler of men. He raised a shrine there in the forest and honored it with flowers and incense. Then he took the monkey's skull from the ashes, and when he returned to his city, he built another shrine to hold it, and there he honored it all his life. And he became a great and wise ruler, loved and honored by his people.

On things that crawl my love is shed
On biped and on quadruped,
On those with many feet.

May crawling things do me no harm;
May those that run with feet along
Do no offence to me.

All creatures that have life within
And all our sentient kith and kin,
May you from every hurt be free
And live beside us peacefully!

—*from the Culla Vagga*

THE RISE OF BUDDHISM

It seems extraordinary that great spiritual teachers, like the Buddha and Jesus, were willing to entrust their teaching to the spoken word and to leave this world, to which they gave their lives, without using the more lasting and reliable form of writing, which was available to both of them. They had complete faith in what they taught. "The Dharma which I have taught you will be your teacher when I have gone," said the Buddha. "The words that I have spoken to you are spirit and life," said Jesus. They also must have had faith in humanity and known that there would always be someone who understood their teaching in its purity and would keep it alive, however it might be distorted and however their forthright and uncompromising message might be softened and elaborated to meet the needs and the longings of the vast majority of people. And they were right, of course: a religion would die if there were not an invisible but unbroken current of its saints from the time of its founding to the present day. Hinduism has proved itself in the lives of Gandhi, Ramakrishna, Vínoba, and many others; Buddhism is very much alive today, in spite of many changes and many elaborations of its doctrine.

After the Buddha died, his disciples met together and held a council, in order to define and recite his teaching. There is no reliable record of this council except tradition, but this is accepted by scholars as true. Five hundred of his followers assembled at his favorite city, Rajagriha, in the present state of Bihar, and met for several months on the Vulture's Peak, by the mouth of a great cave. Their purpose was to recite not only the whole doctrine, beginning with the Four Noble Truths, but the long and detailed rules of the order, the rules of life for lay members, and the principal thoughts and sermons of the Master during the forty-five years of his ministry. All of these were known by heart to many of the monks who were present, and they shared in the long recital.

It is said that the lovable Ananda knew more than anyone else; but it was well known that, in spite of his devotion and conscientiousness, he had not yet reached nirvana, perhaps because he was too much attached to his Master. So he was not allowed at first to join the assembly. But in order to continue his service, even after the Buddha's death, he strove mightily all one night and at dawn reached enlightenment. He was admitted at once and was the most useful member of that company, although he had to confess to a few sins, one being that he had persuaded the Blessed One to admit women to the order. Many of the monks were still unwilling to believe that women were able to live the monastic life.

Scenes from the Buddha's life. A Tibetan painting, eighteenth-nineteenth century. *(Courtesy, Museum of Fine Arts, Boston)*

These five hundred men and many more remembered their Master's commandment to "Go forth for the gain of many, for the welfare of many, in compassion for the world. Preach the glorious doctrine; proclaim the life of holiness." They obeyed, and Buddhism increased in India. It must be remembered that *Buddhism* is a Western term; to the faithful it is the Dharma (in the Buddha's own language, Pali, it is *Dhamma*), the Law, or the Truth. It grew and spread from eastern India to the west and to the south, and existed side by side with Hinduism, from which it had grown. The Brahmins were not pleased to have a strong new sect which denied their traditional authority, but there was no serious quarrel between them, though there were probably many debates. There were so many schools already that one more made little difference.

There were disagreements, however, among the Buddhists themselves and different interpretations of the teaching. A second council was held about a hundred years after the Buddha's death, and at that one there was a cleavage, for a large group of monks walked out and formed another council. They wanted to soften the severity of the monastic rules: to eat after midday, to have more comfortable beds, to handle money. This was the first serious division.

A third council was held in the third century B.C. at the court of the great king Asoka, one of the few rulers who was able to hold the vast extent of northern India together. He was converted to Buddhism after waging a cruel war in order to enlarge his empire. After that he forswore all violence, and during his long reign (270–233 B.C.) he did all that he could to promote the faith and to live by it. He became an example of the old ideal of the Hindu king, whose worth was measured by the welfare of his people. Since he was not a monk but a lay member of the order, he was concerned mostly with the moral teaching of the Master. He built many monasteries and encouraged the monks in their missionary work. He also inscribed in stone, either on rock or on carved pillars, the teaching of the Buddha, his own deeds in obedience to that teaching, and exhortations to all his subjects to do the same. This praiseworthy habit has preserved many of his inscriptions to the present day.

"Thus says His Majesty," one of them reads. "Father and mother must be obeyed; all living creatures must be respected; the teacher must be revered by the student; the truth must be spoken. This is the ancient nature of piety; this leads to length of days and according to this men must act."

"All men are my children," says another. "As I desire that all my children may partake of all that is good and happy in this world and the next, so I desire it for all mankind."

He urged everyone to care for the public welfare: to dig wells, to plant trees, to build shelters for travelers and holy men, to plant healing herbs for medicine, to be kind to servants and to the poor and to animals. He forbade the sacrifice of animals. He also raised stone monuments to mark important places or to commemorate deeds or people. A pillar that marked the birthplace of the Buddha was found very recently, and other monuments of Asoka's have helped archaeologists to find both the sites and the dates of obscure events in Indian history.

One of the most important things that he did was to send missionaries far and wide. Buddhism became not only the most favored faith in India but was established in Ceylon, in the Deccan, and as far north as Kashmir. In his enthusiasm he sent missionaries to the Greek lands on the northwest; indeed, he would have liked to convert the whole world. His most successful mission was to Ceylon: his son, a monk, went there, converted the king, and soon spread the news of the Dharma over that beautiful island. It has been maintained there ever since, and he is revered as its founder. One of Asoka's daughters had become a nun. She followed her brother and brought with her a precious gift: a branch of the very Bo tree—the tree of wisdom—under which the Buddha sat during the night of enlightenment. The branch was successfully transplanted and still flourishes among the ruins of what once was the splendid capital city of the island. It is the oldest historic tree in the world. Ceylon nobly repaid its debt to Buddhism. For the first time, about four hundred years after the Buddha's death, the scriptures were written down and faithfully copied and preserved by the island monks.

Asoka's empire diminished and then broke up, not long after his death. Only a very powerful ruler could hold together such a vast land, and it was now open on the northwest to any invader.

The great civilizations of Asia grew up in the river valleys of the south and of the east. The center of the vast continent was dry, full of deserts and high mountains; agriculture was very difficult, and the people were nomads, living on great herds of sheep and cattle. In the early centuries B.C. they began to invade the richer countries, first to rob and destroy, then to conquer. They were known first as Scythians, then as Huns, Mongols, Turks, and Tatars, and they plagued both Asia and Eastern Europe for two thousand years. It is convenient to speak of them as Tatars.

They came into India over the northwestern passes and conquered and settled there. Their religion was a primitive and barbarous one, and they gladly adopted the

Buddhism that they found in India. A powerful dynasty of these Tatars was formed about the beginning of the Christian era, and one of its kings, Kanishka, was as devoted a Buddhist as Asoka himself. From northwestern India the Dharma was carried into the kingdoms of Central Asia.

The heyday of Buddhism in India was from about 400 B.C. to about A.D. 400. It was a very vigorous time for Hinduism, too, as the reader may remember. The epic stories were composed and written down, and the Bhagavad Gita as well. The fresh vigor of Buddhist thought challenged the Hindus; schools of philosophy flourished and culminated in the Vedanta, which was founded on the Upanishads.

During the centuries just after the Christian era, Buddhism was deeply divided into two schools, one of which followed the original teaching of the Buddha, while the other took that teaching as a foundation for many new ideas and much further thought. The latter school called itself the *Mahayana: yana* means a vehicle and *maha* means great in Sanskrit, from the same root as the Latin *magna.* The Buddha had likened his teaching to a raft which took travelers across a great river to the "other shore." The meaning of vehicle was the same: the Great Vehicle, its followers said, could carry the whole world to salvation. They called the other school the *Hinayana* or Small Vehicle, for they said that only monks who took up the homeless life could be saved by it and that they saved only themselves.

The Hinayanists denied this, quite rightly, because the followers of the Buddha, during the centuries just after his death, had obeyed his command to go forth and teach the Dharma. It was they who had spread the word all over India, into Central Asia, into Ceylon, and later into Burma and Southeast Asia. All this was done before there was any division and before the Mahayana appeared. Not only monks but also many householders had become devoted Buddhists; Asoka was an outstanding example. They naturally did not like the title of Small Vehicle; they called themselves the *Theravada,* or school of the elders. For they had preserved the original records of the Buddha's sermons and teachings; they had written these down in their Master's own language, Pali, and took them as their scriptures. The Mahayanists wrote in Sanskrit and created their own literature and their own scriptures, with many new ideas and variations.

The two schools are sometimes called the southern and the northern schools because the Hinayana prevailed in the south while the Mahayana was carried northward into China, Tibet, Korea, and Japan, and had far-reaching influence in those countries. We shall use the latter terms since they are most commonly known and will be found in other books if the reader cares to explore further this extremely interesting field.

The religious teaching of the Buddha was simple, apart from its philosophical aspects. The Hinayana taught and followed it, and it appealed to many people, but not by any means to all. The Master had been silent about the very things that fascinated the Hindu scholars: the infinite, the real and the unreal, the nature of the universe and of man. He had said very little about nirvana, the final goal of life. For ordinary people, too, his doctrine was kind but stern. He had shown them the way; they must work out their own salvation; there was no one to help them except some wise human teacher. Nonetheless there is a deep desire in people's hearts to worship and to depend on some power higher than themselves and to give that power a human shape so that it seems near and can be appealed to for help and guidance.

THE MAHAYANA

In those creative centuries at the beginning of the Christian era, Buddhist philosophers and writers of the Mahayana school added much to the Dharma that would satisfy the desires of the mind and the heart. Some of their doctrine seems far removed from the Buddha's teaching, but these men held that he had said many things that had not been written down. They said that he had told the partial truth to those who were not able to understand the whole, and that he had taught far more to some of his disciples than to others. They quoted a well-known story:

One day the Buddha was sitting with some of his followers in a grove of trees where they often gathered. He picked up a handful of leaves and asked them, "How many leaves do I hold in my hand, compared to those that are in this wood?" "Compared to those that are on these trees," answered one of them, "the Blessed One holds very few leaves in his hands." "Even so," said the Master, "compared with the truths that I have learned, those that I have told you are very few."

The Mahayanists claimed that they were now making known some of those further truths, even though they were writing many hundreds of years after the Buddha's death. They held that he had not vanished into nirvana when he left this life. He had three appearances or bodies: the human one, when he walked on earth; then a glorified body; finally he had an eternal one, beyond all form and human perception. In his glorified body he still appeared to gods and to enlightened men and continued to teach them.

And who could gainsay them? The talks and sermons that the Buddha had given to his disciples had not been written down for four hundred years. Who could prove that they were any more authentic than those that were written a few centuries later? The Mahayanists used the old formula, "Thus have I heard," and put the new ideas into the Buddha's own mouth. Thus an enormous literature was assembled, which forms the scriptures of the Great Vehicle.

One of these new thoughts is that the visible world of life and death—*samsara*—is no different from nirvana; they are two aspects of the same reality. This idea is expressed in a small book called *The Awakening of Faith:*

> Both aspects are so closely related that one cannot be separated from the other; . . . the mortal and the immortal coincide with one another . . . This can best be illustrated by the water and the waves that are stirred up on the ocean. The water is the same and yet not the same as the waves. The waves are stirred up by the wind, yet the water remains the same. When the wind ceases, the waves subside, but the water remains the same. The wind is ignorance; wisdom is the knowledge that water and waves are one.

Therefore one need not flee from life or fear samsara, as the Buddha had taught; nirvana can be realized in the midst of life.

The Mahayana teaches that there is a still higher goal to be reached than nirvana. All men, all living creatures, possess the very same nature as the Buddha himself and can become enlightened even as he did. Indeed, the whole creation—plants and trees, rocks and grass, even grains of dust—is moving toward perfection, to Buddhahood.

When the doors of the mind were thrown open as widely as this, that rich imagination, which is one of India's great gifts, had free play. Soon there were millions of Buddhas in millions of worlds, working for the freedom and salvation of all living creatures. The Buddha Gótama, who had trodden the roads of India, was one of many, and sometimes even he was overshadowed by other figures. These became the gods of Buddhism, replacing the Hindu deities.

One of the most important is the Buddha Amitabha, the Buddha of Boundless Light. Aeons ago, it was said, he had been a man who attained great spiritual power after innumerable lives. He was on the very threshold of nirvana, but he vowed that he would go no further until he was sure that any person who called upon his name with perfect faith, especially at the moment of death, would be reborn in his paradise without further reincarnation. His vow was honored; he entered nirvana and became a Buddha. His paradise, the Pure Land, lies in the west and is more sumptuous than the heaven of Indra. In the Pure Land the leaves and flowers of innumerable trees are made of jewels of every color; on quiet lakes grow lotuses as large as chariot wheels, of every lovely hue. Birds sing, and music flows from the clouds and from streams of bells hung between the trees. "And if they desire a palace . . . adorned with a hundred thousand gates made with different jewels, covered with heavenly flowers, full of couches strewn with beautiful cushions, then just such a palace appears before them. And there they dwell, play, sport, and walk about, honored and surrounded by seven times seven thousand of dancing nymphs." (What would Shariputra have thought of that, he who with his great toe had set the whole palace of Indra to shaking and trembling?)

Amitabha himself comes to the dying one and takes him to this lovely land. If he is already a good and devout man who believes in the Mahayana doctrine, he finds himself seated upon a jeweled lotus on one of the crystal lakes, in the presence of Amitabha and many other spiritual beings. Very soon he becomes completely enlightened, and all the celestial worlds are open to him. If he is not very good and is not purified of his sins, he is enclosed in a lotus bud which will not open until he is able to understand the doctrine and start on the path of enlightenment. Sometimes the lotus bud opens in a few weeks, sometimes not for long ages, according to the worthiness of its prisoner.

This belief presents a kind god and a life of bliss and pleasure after death; it also restores the ego, the personality that the Buddha denied; for who is it that enjoys the Pure Land if not the one who calls upon Amitabha? That very person survives to live forever in paradise.

Since there are so many Buddhas there must also be many people who are on their way to becoming Buddhas, who are, in one holy life after another, nearing their full awakening. Such a person is called a Bodhisattva, which means literally one whose being (*sattva*) is wisdom or enlightenment (*bodhi*). The Buddha, before his night under the Bo tree, was a Bodhisattva; he was a Bodhisattva through all the legendary birth stories that are told about him. Only after full enlightenment does one become a Buddha.

Now, with the Mahayana, another new belief arose, whence and when no one knows: there are Bodhisattvas who have reached nirvana but who have refused to pass into that state of bliss, as Amitabha had done. They have chosen to remain in the world out of love and pity for suffering humanity and have vowed that they will liberate all men before they themselves will accept the infinite peace and freedom that awaits them. When the Buddha died, it was believed that he entered nirvana and was beyond all prayer or appeal, except to a very few who claimed to behold his glorified body. But the Bodhisattvas are here, on the hither side of heaven, full of kindness, ready to help, for that is their whole purpose. Most of

A Chinese image of the Bodhisattva Kuan-yin. Carved and painted wood. *(William Rockhill Nelson Gallery of Art)*

them have once been human beings, but there are others who are simply embodiments of wisdom, mercy, or contemplation. They are thought of as radiant beings, invisible but ever present. They are gods, but they are a new kind of god, with no problems of their own, pure of heart, stainless of mind, possessed of all knowledge and of infinite love.

There are countless portrayals of these lovely beings, in paintings and sculptures, in China and Tibet, Korea and Japan. They are exquisite and graceful figures, sometimes seated in the classic pose of meditation, with legs crossed, or with one foot resting on the opposite knee; or standing, with their two, or many, hands holding out gifts and blessings. They seem to sway or bend toward the worshiper; their faces are serene; they are crowned and hung with jewels. They are revered by millions of people and are powerful forces for good. As Buddhism spread northwestward into the Tatar kingdoms of Central Asia and into Tibet, primitive peoples, who believed in both good and evil spirits and in savage gods, replaced their fearful images with those of the gracious Bodhisattvas, and their fears were calmed by the assurance of an infinite and loving compassion.

Since every creature possesses the Buddha nature, anyone with enough devotion and perseverance can become a Bodhisattva, though the way is arduous. The qualities that one must possess, first of all, are six: charity, virtue, forebearance, zeal, meditation, and finally wisdom, or that intuitive insight to which the other five lead. Then the aspirant must take the four vows of a Bodhisattva: to save all beings; to destroy all evil passions; to learn the truth and teach it to others; to lead all beings to Buddhahood.

The Mahayana is rightly called the Great Vehicle, for it appeals to every sort of person. To many it gives comfort and the promise of a happy afterlife. To the spiritually-minded, it offers the noble purpose of the Bodhisattva, and, if one is able to attain it, the bliss of Buddhahood. It also attracts the learned; for various schools of Mahayana philosophy have speculated upon those things that the Buddha left unsaid. Like the Hindus, they sought an infinite reality, beyond what seemed to them the unreality of the visible world. They gave it a new name, the Void. This does not mean emptiness in the usual sense of the word, but simply that which is devoid of those qualities that we perceive with our senses or grasp with our minds. Many profound and subtle books were written, and many different schools of philosophy and sects of the Dharma developed, based upon one book or another, for there was no final authority, such as the Vedas.

The Four Great Vows

However innumerable beings are, I vow to save them;
However inexhaustible the passions are, I vow to extinguish them;
However immeasurable the Dharmas are, I vow to master them;
However incomparable the Buddha-truth is, I vow to attain it.

Buddhism and Hinduism lived side by side for over a thousand years in India. Each influenced the other, and they became so much alike that it was hard to distinguish them. The doctrine of the Mahayana that every creature possesses the Buddha nature is the same that was taught in the Upanishads; the same that the father taught his son: "It is the subtle essence of all things. That is the Truth; That is the Self. And you, my son—you are That."

Buddhism declined in India from about the sixth

century on. A Chinese pilgrim, traveling in the seventh century, writes with sorrow of the ruins of monasteries and temples. By about 1000, little was left of it, and that little was savagely destroyed by the Muslim invasions of that period. Unlike the Hindus, the Muslims were fanatically intolerant; their God was the only God and the teaching of their prophet Muhammad must be forced upon people if they would not accept it willingly. They also forbade the worship of any graven image, as the Jews also did. Therefore, as they swept into northern India, they destroyed the rich sculpture and painting that they found there, razed the temples and monasteries, and massacred the monks.

The Dharma took refuge in the countries outside of India where its missionaries and its teachers had gone, and where it was eagerly welcomed.

Buddhism of the Hinayana school became the most important religion of Ceylon and of the countries of Southeast Asia, where it remains now. It spread also into Indonesia. The Mahayana faith was carried first into the Tatar kingdoms on the northwestern borders of India and then into China, Tibet, Korea, and Japan. In China and Japan it was accepted on equal terms with the strong religions already established there. In China an important sect, the Zen, was developed, which will be discussed in the next chapter, for it owes much to the character and ways of thinking of the Chinese.

In Tibet Buddhism permeated the whole life of the people; it was not only their religion but their government, for the Dalai Lama, the head of the church, also ruled the state. The missionaries who carried the Dharma into foreign countries always adapted it to whatever religion they found there. The Tibetan religion was superstitious and full of gods and demons. The land is a high and rugged one of immense empty spaces, towering mountains, and extremes of weather; the forces of nature are not always benevolent. Tibetan Buddhism incorporated some of the superstitions, but it also produced many wise and holy men, who lived either as hermits in the mountains or in the many monasteries that crown the hills. In 1950 Tibet was taken over by the Chinese Communists who would put an end, if they could, to all religions. The Dalai Lama has taken refuge in India.

Buddhism remains, strong and serene, in several Asian countries; it has returned to India and has adherents in many Western lands, for it is open to everyone and does not belong to any place or people.

Collared crows on winter prunus. A Chinese painting on silk, early sixteenth century. *(The Metropolitan Museum of Art, Fletcher Fund, 1947)*

PART FOUR

The Religions of China

The blind musicians
In the courtyard of Chou
Have set up their pillars and crossbars
With upright plumes and hooks for the drums
and the bells;
The small and large drums are hanging there,
The tambourines, the stone chimes, the batons
and tiger clappers.
When all have been struck the music begins;
Then the pipes and the flutes sound shrilly.
Sweet is the music,
Sweet as the song of birds.
The ancestors listen;
They are our guests;
Forever and ever they gaze upon our victories.
—from the Shi King, The Book of Songs

The Chinese people are different in many ways from the Indians, and their religion has a different emphasis. They are like the Indians in that they found themselves in possession of rich river valleys and a vast land into which they could spread as their population increased. As far as they know, the Chinese originated north of the Yellow River, the Hwang Ho, in the present provinces of Shensi and Shansi. Consequently they have a deep and abiding contact with and feeling for the earth they live on, a feeling which most civilized people, who have moved again and again, cannot share. The mountains and the rivers, the land and the grain, earth and heaven, were worshiped by them for thousands of years, until the beginning of the present century and perhaps now. The four seasons, the four directions, the movements of the sun, moon, and stars, were like aspects of their own being.

Their civilization is a very old one, for it goes back beyond 3000 B.C. They are the only people in the world today whose culture has remained for so long in its own land. Their long history has often been stormy and broken by periods of devastating invasion or rebellion; twice they were conquered by their perennial enemies, the Tatars of Central Asia, but their alien rulers conformed to the Chinese culture, which was much more advanced than their own. There were no more magnificent and more Chinese emperors than those of the Manchu (a Tatar) Dynasty in the seventeenth and eighteenth centuries. (Because of its length, Chinese history is usually divided, not into centuries, but into dynasties; a dynasty is a succession of rulers all belonging to one family. The word is also used to denote the time during which those rulers were in power.) The nation survived disasters that might have destroyed weaker societies; it had long centuries of peace and production and is still powerful today.

What has caused this unique and enduring life? A Western writer, who lived many years in China and worked and studied with Chinese scholars, has said," . . . these results, so long enduring and so vast, must be owing to the social and the political life of the Chinese being founded on great and eternal truths."[1] What are these truths?

Like the Indians, and all other early peoples, the Chinese, at first, felt around them powers far greater than themselves and localized them as different aspects of nature. But above all they recognized a supreme power which they sometimes called Heaven and sometimes the Supreme Lord. It was never given a form or an image, but it was believed to have a benevolent will and purpose and to care about its creation. It was what we express in the one word—God.

This was an intuitive feeling that became a belief; later, as their minds developed, they sought an explanation of the cause and creation of the universe they found themselves in. They explained it this way: there was originally a Great Unity (another word for God, or the Absolute) and from it came forth two breaths or forces whose interplay created the "ten thousand things," as they called the visible universe. These two forces are the opposite elements that make up our world, without which we could not perceive anything: bright and dark, hard and soft, active and passive, light and heavy. We could not see objects if there were not both brightness and shadow; we could not hear if there were not both sound and silence; we could not stand or move if there were not both weight and lightness. These oppositions can be multiplied indefinitely and are the warp and woof of our earthly life. The Great Unity alone has no opposite.

This seems to have been a very early idea, although it

was not fully developed for many centuries. For the earliest of mythical rulers, whose name was Fu Hi, went up to the top of a mountain and sacrificed there to the Supreme Lord. It is also told of him that he saw a tortoise climbing out of a river, and on its back he made out diagrams and lines in which he read this explanation of life. In these diagrams there were two kinds of lines, broken — —, and unbroken ——, which symbolized the two breaths, and in their combinations he saw the interplay that brought forth the ever-changing flow of life. It is easy to see lines and designs on the carapace of a tortoise, which ever after was considered a holy creature.

Different words have been used in speaking of the two forces. At first they were called the bright and the dark, or the firm and the yielding, but the most familiar words are the Chinese *Yin* and *Yang,* which were given to them in later times. Yin is the dark, the quiet, the unifying element, symbolized by the earth, the moon, water, and so forth. Yang is the bright, the active, the transforming power, symbolized by the sun, by fire, by the sky. Yang is male, and Yin is female. Fu Hi's unbroken line is Yang; the broken line is Yin. Later, when the Chinese became great artists, the whole cosmic idea was embodied in another symbol:

The circle represents the Great Unity, the two inner divisions of it the Yang and the Yin. Note that these are equal and in perfect harmony. Good and evil are not among the opposites: both Yang and Yin are good; evil only appears when the harmony between them is disturbed, and one dominates the other. If on earth the Yang got out of hand, there would be storms and tempests and fires; if the Yin predominated, nothing would grow, and the waters might rise in another great flood. So, in human life, man and wife must complement each other and live in harmony; although, it must be said, the Yang was always superior, as the sun is to the moon or the heavens to the earth. In each one of them there is a bit of the other.

The Chinese were much concerned with nature, partly because they were an agricultural people and therefore dependent upon sun and rain and the changes of the seasons. They were careful observers of the heavens, from very early times, and found the North Star, the zodiac, recognized five planets, and before long predicted eclipses. In the movements of these heavenly bodies and the rhythm of the seasons, in the unceasing flow of life and change, they perceived an order and harmony which was beneficial to all creatures. Since the Supreme Lord, or Heaven, was in charge of all this, order and harmony must be the Way of Heaven, the will of God. This way is called the *Tao** and is translated in so many ways that the Chinese word will be used hereafter in this book, as will the two words Yin and Yang.

Man's life was a very important part of the universe he perceived; therefore his life, too, should be orderly and harmonious; he should live, as the heavenly bodies did, according to the Tao. Men were given their nature by Heaven; therefore it was good. Five virtues were inherent in it: kindness (in its widest sense), righteousness, right behavior, wisdom, and good faith. Men were led astray by circumstances, by temptations and ignorance; but if they were taught and guided by those who understood and if they were justly governed, they would live in peace and

*pronounced dow, rhyming with now

comfort. Those who understood, whose business it was to teach and to govern, had a great responsibility. Man is the only creature who knows about the divine workings; therefore he is responsible even for nature; for if his conduct breaks the harmony of life, disasters such as flood or drought may follow. The moral code of the Chinese was based on this belief.

THE FIVE RELATIONSHIPS

The moral code is very unusual in one respect. Most religions are concerned with the individual person, his relation to God, and in consequence his relations with other people. For those who care most about their faith, the first is often the most important, especially in the East. The Hindu goes into the forest to meditate and to find union with Brahman; the Buddhist goes into the monastery to attain nirvana. Both leave behind them all human relationships, save that, perhaps, of teacher to disciple.

The Chinese took the opposite way. Having decided what they believed about the universe and man, they turned almost all of their attention to human relationships and the building of a happy society. Theirs is the only religion which includes government. Its teaching was directed to two closely related things: the family and the state.

The whole duty of man was set forth in the Five Relationships: those between ruler and subject, father and son, elder brother and younger brother, husband and wife, friend and friend. If these were faithfully carried out, there would be harmony not only in human society but between man and nature and between Heaven and man, for this was the Way of Heaven.

The ruler's relation to his people was that of a father to his children. He must see to it that they had enough food and the other necessities of life; he must guide and teach them how to live in accord with the Tao, and above all he must set them an example by his own life. If this were done, the natural goodness of their nature would develop, and they would hardly know that they were being governed. The least government was the best; the highest praise that could be given to a ruler was to state that in all the land only a dozen men were in prison.

This relationship was far more binding on the ruler than on his subjects. He stood between man and Heaven and was responsible for everything that happened in the country and for the welfare of all creatures, human and nonhuman, that inhabited it. He was known as the Son of Heaven, or the One Man, for he was unique and his position was awe-inspiring. However, if he were unworthy, neglected his duty, or oppressed his subjects, then Heaven would send down calamities. The people would soon know that he had failed them; first they would murmur and then rebel. It was their duty to do so. For the high position of the king (later of the emperor) was given to the office, not necessarily to the man. If he betrayed his trust, he lost the favor of Heaven and became the meanest of men. It was then the duty of some strong and enterprising leader to overthrow him and to start a new dynasty. This right of rebellion was written into the very scriptures of China, and it was often claimed. A wise king of one of the early dynasties said to his ministers, "Do not dare to suppress the remonstrances of the people." "Heaven loves the people," the Book of History says. "Heaven hears as the people hear; it sees as the people see."[2]

One of the duties of a ruler was to choose wise and able ministers. The scriptures of China, which correspond to the Vedas or the Bible, are known as the Five Classics, and one of these is the Book of History, which carries one back to legendary times, nearly 3000 B.C. From the very beginning it was constantly emphasized that the ruler should choose men of virtue and ability, no matter who they were; he should not have favorites or give high positions to members of his family. One of the much-revered legendary kings said to his chief councilor, "What are ministers? They are my legs and arms, my ears and eyes. I wish to help and support the people; you carry out my wishes. I wish to spread the harmony of my government to the four quarters of the earth; you are my agent. When I do wrong, it is you who must correct me."[3]

A young king, anxious to find a worthy minister, dreamed that he saw the man he needed and sent messengers out to search for him, with a picture of the man he had dreamed about. They found him, a builder, living in a wild part of the land. The king made him his chief minister and kept him at his side. "Morning and evening teach me to be virtuous," he said. "I am a weapon of steel; you are my whetstone. I am crossing a great stream; you are my boat with its oars. I am in a year of great drought; you are a copious rain. Open your mind and enrich mine. Be like medicine that must pain the patient in order to cure him. So I may tread in the steps of my great ancestor and give peace to the millions of the people."[4]

It has been said before that legends are important because they reveal the ideals and desires of a people. The legendary heroes of China are not warriors or conquerors or resplendent rulers; they are humble and wise kings who care for the welfare of their people and who listen to them.

The king's ministers might come from any place or family, rich or poor, for there was no rigid class system. Men were graded according to their occupations: scholar, farmer, artisan, and merchant, in that order. The scholar was always most honored, and the government of China became a government of scholars. There was no ruler or warrior class. There are many stories in the later histories

A Confucian official. Carved and painted wood, Ming Dynasty, 1368-1644. *(The Metropolitan Museum of Art, Fletcher Fund, 1934)*

(for the Chinese were faithful and diligent historians) of ministers who risked or suffered a very unpleasant death because they would not obey their ruler or because they told him that he was doing wrong.

There was one great tyrant who, after a long period of division and misrule, brought the whole country under his sway and unified it. This was a good thing, but he did it with great cruelty, and he would not listen to anyone. There were, of course, people who opposed him, and he heard that his own mother was conspiring with them. He sent her away from his court and killed all those, with their families, who plotted against him. Then he sat on his throne with his sword across his knees and said that anyone who disagreed with him would be killed. It is said that twenty-seven of his ministers and officials came fearlessly to him and told him that he was doing wrong, for banishing one's mother and refusing to listen to advice were two unforgivable faults in a ruler. They were all put to death.

Then an old man who had served him well came to him and stood before his throne. "Your Majesty has a violent and presumptuous character," he said, "and will not listen to the advice of virtuous men. The people will hear of this and will not respect you. I fear for your dynasty." He had no doubt that he would be promptly executed, but the tyrant realized that there was truth in these words; he brought his mother back from exile and asked the old man to be his councilor.

There are many such stories, and wise and courageous ministers have been honored as much as great emperors. This tradition lasted up to the present century when the last, dying dynasty of imperial China was in the hands of a powerful and ignorant woman, the Empress Dowager. She tried to make war on all the powers of Europe that were pressing in upon China. When she gave a stupid and disastrous order to kill all foreigners in the country, two of her ministers disobeyed and changed the order to "Protect all foreigners." They were both beheaded and died with serene courage.

In such a long history there was every kind of ruler and every kind of minister, good and bad, strong and weak, corrupt and upright. But the ideal remained, strong and steadfast, for forty or fifty centuries, and where there is an ideal, it can be appealed to, and the appeal is a powerful one.

The next relationship was equally important and was often put first; it was closely connected with government. It was the relation between parent and child, particularly between father and son. On the father's side it consisted of love and care as long as he lived; on the son's it consisted of reverence and obedience during and after his father's lifetime. This relation was, of course, extended to grandparents and great-grandparents, and, on the father's part, to his descendants. It was also extended, in lessening intensity, to all the elders of the family and to old people in general, for it was believed that old people accumulated wisdom with experience and should be honored. Old trees and rocks and mountains were honored for the same reason.

The family was the social unit, as it was in some other countries, but in China it was more carefully organized and more important than elsewhere. If a family was well-to-do, all the male members of it lived together all their lives, in a large compound; the girls, when they married, became a part of their husbands' families. The houses, mostly of one story, were built around courtyards, each married couple having its own court and rooms. There was always a garden, as large and beautiful as the family could afford, for Chinese gardens are as beautiful as any in the world, and the courtyards, too, had flowers and blossoming plants or trees. The oldest man was the head and ruler of the household; his sons and grandsons brought their brides to the house and raised their children there, unless business or government duty took them elsewhere. If it did, their wives and children usually stayed behind in the family home. There were often four or even five generations and sometimes fifty or sixty people living in the rambling compound, for servants and occasionally slaves lived there, too, and were accounted members of the household. All the property was held in common, and all family matters were decided by the council of elders, headed by the oldest one. In the villages, each farming family lived in the same way. In poorer houses, there was probably only one courtyard, and sometimes each family had only one room rather than its own apartment. All the sons worked the land together, and all earnings were held in common.

The duty of a son to his father and his mother did not end with their death. The Chinese, like the Egyptians, made much of death; the funeral and the ceremonies of mourning were as elaborate as the family could afford. It was believed that dead persons did not cease to be concerned about their families; that their spirits remained not far away and protected and blessed their descendants. In return, however, they must be honored and nourished not only with reverence and affection but with food, whose essence they breathed, as gods are supposed to do, while the grosser part was eaten later by those who offered it. In any large house there was an ancestral hall, in the place of honor, facing south, where offerings were made. There, in each season and on many other occasions, food and wine were presented, candles were lighted and incense burned, while the members of the family bowed down to the ground before their ancestors. Their spirits were represented by rectangular tablets of wood, high and narrow, on which the name of each ancestor was carved or drawn in the beautiful Chinese characters, which are written vertically, not horizontally as ours are. The tablets stood upright on a pedestal of wood and were often finely carved. It was believed that the spirits came when they were summoned to the feast and were actually present in the tablets that bore their names. In this hall every newborn son was presented to his forebears, and when any important event happened to the household, it was announced to them there.

In smaller houses a room was set aside for the ancestral tablets and similar offerings were made; in a poor house the tablets were set on a shelf in the main room. In villages sometimes the whole population had the same surname and was descended from the same ancestor. If that was so, there was a temple in which everyone assembled at certain times and made their offerings, as well as in their homes. From the emperor to the poorest peasant this custom prevailed, from the earliest times we know of until the present century.

This feeling for their forefathers had a deep and lasting effect on the behavior of all the people. A man was proud to do well in the world and to be virtuous because in doing so he honored and pleased his ancestors as well as his present family. If he did wrong, he brought disgrace upon them and lost their protection and blessing for himself and his children. He was also disapproved of by the family with whom he lived so intimately and by his neighbors and friends, so that life was a misery.

The family system has been a potent police force as well. If a man injured another, the two families settled the affair; if a man got into debt, the family paid it but saw to it that the offender repaid the common fund. The father or the eldest member had the power of life and death: if a very terrible crime was committed, the criminal could be put to death; or he could be expelled from the home, and then where was he? A man without home or parents, without son or ancestor, was lost indeed. The family both judged and protected him, and he usually chose to live in accord with it.

While the first two relationships were the most important, the others were also binding. The eldest brother had an almost paternal attitude to the younger ones, especially if the parents were dead. He felt responsible for them, and they, in turn, deferred and were loyal to him. Husband and wife must live in harmony together, as should the Yang and the Yin. Between friends there should be trust and faithfulness.

This close kinship and the subservience of younger to older may seem confining and intolerable to Western minds, and indeed, it became so to many young Chinese after encountering Western ideas. But it must be remembered that the relationship worked both ways. It was not mere obedience on the part of the younger members of the family, nor was the child the only obedient one. He saw his parents pay the same reverence to their parents that was required of him. His father obeyed the family elder, and that made it quite natural for him, in turn, to obey his father. And he obeyed only insofar as his elders were in the right, for truth and the Way of Heaven came first.

One of the disciples of the great teacher, Confucius, asked him once, "Is it filial for a son to obey every command of his father, whether right or wrong?" "What are you saying!" exclaimed the Master. "When the command is wrong, a son should resist his father and a minister should resist his king. If a father has a son who resists his wrong commands, he will be saved from serious faults. How can he be called filial who obeys when his father tells him to do wrong?" It is said, too, that once, when Confucius was Minister of Crime, a young man was brought before him. He sentenced the young man to prison for the wrongs he had committed, but he put the father in prison, too, for not having taught his son properly.

The children did not have freedom, but they had security, unless there were external misfortunes. In the village, the land belonged as much to each growing son as to anyone else, and the home was also his. A suitable wife was found for him and husbands for the daughters. In richer households it was the same: if there was a family business, the son had a place in it; if there was not enough room for him, other work was found by the family elders. And if any boy, a peasant or a rich man's son, had a good mind, everything was done to give him a good education and to make a scholar of him, for then he might hold a government position, and nothing reflected more honor on a family or on a village than to have one of its members enter government service. There was no barrier of class or wealth; and, since one of the chief duties of those in authority was to watch for able men, he might be employed anywhere from a small official post in his county or province up to the emperor's court, according to his ability.

In addition to these relationships, courtesy and good manners between all people were considered important to the harmony of society. Quarreling and brawling were looked down upon and probably occurred more rarely in China than elsewhere.

THE CEREMONIES

The Five Relationships were to the Chinese religion what the Eightfold Path was to Buddhism or the Ten Commandments to the Jews. They bound the people together and were the foundation of the long and continuous life of their nation and their culture. This was the human side of their faith. There was another equally important one: the relation of man to heaven and to earth, to the seasons, to the sun, moon, and stars, to hills and rivers, and to innumerable spirits.

This relation was expressed through ceremony. There were many ceremonies, starting with simple ones observed by the farmers and workmen who worshiped the gods of the household; they became more elaborate as a man's responsibilities increased, until the life of the king and even that of his officials throughout the country was one great round of ritual. The ceremonies embodied the reverence, the dependence, and the gratitude that were felt toward all the powers of nature and toward Heaven. This last relation was the most important, and the most impressive rite was the one that celebrated it. Only the ruler, the Son of Heaven, could perform it. No temple was raised, and no image was made; the burnt offering of a young bull without blemish and of one color was presented on a raised, open altar just before the dawn of the winter solstice. At that time the light and warmth of the sun are returning to the earth and the Yang, which symbolizes the visible heaven and the sun, is coming into power again, after the Yin of winter and of darkness. It was a ceremony of gratitude to Heaven for the benefits of the past year and of prayer for the year to come. The altar was raised outside the city wall, to the south, and was always round, as Heaven was believed to be. On the north of the city there was a square altar to the Earth, and there at the summer solstice the king worshiped the kindly Earth, on which all life depends.

The seasons were also important, for the first things created by the interplay of Yang and Yin were the five elements—water, fire, earth, metal, and wood—and the four seasons. In the spring the king, followed by all his ministers and courtiers, went out of the eastern gate to welcome the season. Three months later he went to the southern gate to greet the summer; then the autumn at the western gate and the winter at the northern were received as honored presences. As towns and cities grew up, the magistrates in charge of them performed the same ceremonies.

All these rites were observed in elaborate and minute detail, with all the artistry of an intensely artistic people. At the winter solstice the king and his ministers wore dark blue robes, for that was the color of Heaven; blue lanterns lighted the altar, and offerings of blue silk and jade were also burned, so that their essence would rise to Heaven. The Earth's color was yellow, and the offerings were buried, not burned, at the ceremony of the summer solstice. Yellow robes and ornaments were worn, and the king was drawn by yellow horses with black tails. To greet the spring the king wore green robes and green jade ornaments; his chariot bore a green flag. The summer's color was red, the autumn's white, and the winter's black. Every vase and bowl used in the sacrifices, the colors and embroideries of every piece of clothing, the color and harness of the horses and the decorations of the chariots, were in accord with the purpose of the ceremony. The unique beauty of Chinese artistry—the silk, the jade carvings, the porcelain, the innumerable lovely objects that grace our museums—is due to its having meaning and purpose. At the great ceremonies there were also music and stately dancing.

In addition to these seasonal rites, the mountains and the rivers of the realm—indeed, all the sources of that precious element, water—must be worshiped and the royal forefathers were honored in the king's ancestral temple. Every month offerings were made to them; every season a great sacrifice was performed; and every three or five years there was a still more elaborate one. There were also occasional ceremonies: in case of misfortune, such as drought, flood or pestilence, war, the death of a king or a parent, the ancestors and the powers of nature must be informed and their blessing invoked. The king was the high priest of the nation, the mediator between man and Heaven; the oldest male parent was the priest in every household. There were masters of ceremony who conducted the elaborate rites, but there was no professional priesthood.

This rhythmic and ordered way of life was conceived in very early days. The country was small; its ruler was a king, not yet an emperor. He parceled out the ever-increasing territory among trustworthy men, for he could not reach it all himself. This kind of government is known as the feudal system and has been followed in many countries in their early days. The Chinese feudal lords were rulers in their own domains and must observe all the ceremonies except the offering to Heaven. The book that describes and regulates these matters is called the *Li Ki,* the Book of Rites, and is one of the most important of the Five Classics. It was formulated and much of it was written down during the Chou* Dynasty (1122–221 B.C.).

This book says: "The rules of ceremony can be traced to their origin in the Great Unity. While they originated in Heaven, their movement reaches to Earth and their practice to all the business of life. They serve to nourish the nature of man; they are the embodiment of what is right; they supply the channels through which we can understand the Way of Heaven. They form the bond that holds the multitude together. Therefore the wise kings of old knew that the rules of ceremony could not be dispensed

---

*pronounced jo

with, while the ruin of states, the destruction of families and the punishing of individuals are always preceded by the abandonment of these rules."[5]

It must not be thought, however, that life was either solemn or rigid. The Chinese have a great sense of humor and are masters of the arts of pleasure, from their architecture, painting, sculpture, drama, to the no less important arts of costume and cookery. For was it not written in the Book of Rites, "The nature of man cannot be without pleasure"? It could be better enjoyed when life was ordered and each person knew his place.

The religion which has been so briefly sketched here contains those "great and eternal truths" on which the society and culture were founded and which remained with surprisingly little change for such a long time. Both Chinese and Western scholars are apt to say that the Chinese had no religion; that they had only a moral philosophy or an ethical code. This seems a strange statement to make about a people who believed in a supreme power which was benevolent and all-powerful, whose will for man was goodness and harmony; a people who built a high moral code upon this belief and followed it with unusual faithfulness, and whose year was a cycle of worship.

CONFUCIUS

The words in the Book of Rites about the abandonment of the ceremonies were proved true after the Chou Dynasty had ruled for several centuries. It had been founded by noble men of high vision, but after many generations the descendants of these men enjoyed the power and pleasures of the throne rather than its duties. The very growth and prosperity of the country made their rule more difficult. The feudal lords increased their domains toward the south and the west; the lords of the larger states became far more powerful than the king and spent their time fighting with one another and conquering their smaller neighbors. The Five Relationships and the rules of ceremony were forgotten: brother killed brother; ministers betrayed their masters; and some of the princes sacrificed to Heaven as if they were kings. The last four centuries of the Chou Dynasty, from the seventh to the third centuries B.C., were known as the Time of the Warring States.

It was during this turbulent and unhappy time that the great teacher Confucius was born in the state of Lu, in what is now Shantung, an eastern province of China. He was born in 551 B.C. of an honorable family of the name of Kung. His Chinese title is Kung-fu-tze, or Master Kung, but the Latinized name, Confucius, given him by the first European missionaries, is almost always used outside of China.

He was a serious and studious boy and at fifteen, so he tells us, devoted himself to learning, especially the classic books of History, Poetry, Rites, Music, and the Book of Changes. He loved music; he played the lute and sang. Like all scholars, he wanted to serve in the government of his state, and in his youth he held two positions: one as keeper of provisions, the other as overseer of the pastures. It is said that he attained higher positions, finally being made Minister of Crime (or Justice), and that the ruler of a neighboring state became alarmed for fear that Lu, having such a wise councilor, might become too powerful. Therefore he sent beautiful dancers and horses as a gift to the prince of Lu, who forgot his duties and gave himself to pleasure. Confucius did what a true minister should do: when his master ceased to attend to his duties, he resigned his office. He then became what he was most fitted to be—a great teacher.

He saw with sorrow the war and discord all about him, the neglect of duty and of the rites that had held the

Confucius and two of his disciples. A Japanese painting, seventeenth century. *(Courtesy, Museum of Fine Arts, Boston)*

country together. He knew that if the ideals and standards of the holy books were put into practice, as the wise founders of the dynasty had done, all would be well again. So he taught the Five Classics, which he knew so well, and added his own wisdom. He gathered these books together, compiled, and edited them. In his time writing was incised on strips of bamboo, bound together with thongs of leather into clumsy but precious books.

Students gathered about him and became his disciples, honoring him as a sage and revering him as a father. He accepted whoever came to him. "I have never refused to teach anyone," he said, "even if he had only a bundle of dried meat as a fee." But he wanted only those who wished and were able to learn. "I do not display the truth to one who is not eager to know it. When I have presented one corner of a subject to anyone and he cannot make out for himself the other three, I do not repeat the lesson."[6] When he found a student asleep during the daytime, he said, "Rotten wood cannot be carved; one cannot build a wall with dung. Why should I even reprove him?"[7] He appreciated and loved his earnest disciples, and the relation between them was a close one.

Although he was never given the opportunity to do all that he wanted to do in government, several of his disciples were given important posts, some in Lu, some in neighboring states, where they distinguished themselves. One of them heard that people were saying that he was greater than Confucius. "Let me compare our stature to a wall around a house," he said. "My wall reaches to a man's shoulders; anyone may look over it and see whatever is within. My master's wall is fathoms high; if one cannot find a door and enter it, he cannot know the beauties that lie within; and few find the door." He also heard that a courtier was speaking evil of his master. "It is of no use to do that," he said. "My master cannot be reviled. The talents and virtues of other men are like mounds and hillocks; he is like the sun or the moon, which cannot be stepped over. What harm can anyone do to him?"[8]

Confucius had no new doctrine to preach. "I am a transmitter and not a maker," he said. "I love and believe in the ancient sages."[9] These were the legendary kings and the founders of the Chou Dynasty; it was the wisdom of the Five Classics that he wished to transmit. He was honored in his own state, and his fame spread abroad, but he was never given a position in which he could influence or transform the government as he longed to do. He left Lu, therefore, when he was in his fifties and visited other states, traveling in his carriage and accompanied by some of his followers. He was received hospitably everywhere he went, and his counsel was sought by rulers and statesmen, but nowhere was he asked to take over their government. The feudal princes preferred to go on doing just as they pleased. Disappointed and feeling himself a failure, he returned at last to Lu and died quietly there when he was seventy-two years old. His tomb stands in his native town, close by the splendid temple that was built in his honor and which is guarded by his descendants of the eightieth generation.

He once gave a very brief account of his life: "At fifteen I set my heart on learning; at thirty I stood firm; at forty I had no doubts; at fifty I understood the Way of Heaven; at sixty I obeyed it; at seventy I could follow my own desires and do no wrong."[10] This was the mark of the sage: that he so completely gave himself to the Tao that it worked through him and everything he did was right with no effort or decision of his own. It would have warmed his heart to know that after his death he was considered the equal of the great men whom he admired so much and that he was ranked as the last of the great sages.

Although he wrote nothing but a brief chronicle of his state, Lu, the sayings and teachings of Confucius were cherished by his disciples and written down by them after he died. They exist in a book called the *Analects* (or Conversations) and in two short treatises called "The Doctrine of the Mean" and "The Great Learning," which were, in later centuries, added to the Five Classics and equally honored. They are called the Four Books, for another was added, written by Mencius, the greatest follower of Confucius. He says in the first treatise:

"Integrity is the Way of Heaven. He who possesses it does what is right without effort and understands without thinking; he naturally and easily embodies the Way. He who chooses what is good and holds fast to it, attains integrity. In order to do this, he must study intensively what is good, inquire about it, think carefully about it, and earnestly practice it.

"Only the man who has complete integrity can fully develop his own nature. If he can develop it fully he can develop that of other men and that of animals and all living things. Therefore he can take part in the transforming and nourishing powers of Heaven and Earth and is one with them."[11]

Integrity means wholeness, whole-heartedness, completeness. The man of integrity depends on nothing outside himself; people and circumstances cannot harm or disturb his inner security. "The wise man has no doubts; the virtuous man has no anxiety; the brave man has no fear. . . . The wise man is content and composed; the foolish man is full of troubles."

"Is there one rule which a man could live by for his whole life?" asked a student of the Master.

"What you do not want done to yourself do not do to others," answered Confucius. "The good man who wishes to provide for himself will provide for others; if he wishes to better himself, he will better others. This is the underlying principle of my teaching."[12]

These wise words were for the individual. The next consideration, of course, was good government, which the Chinese have always known to be necessary for human happiness and welfare. Confucius held to the old principle: that the example of the ruler was the most important element in government. "The Great Learning" consists of a few succinct paragraphs that contain this teaching.

He says, in effect, that the wise men of old who wished to rule the whole country virtuously first put their own states in order. To do this, they first regulated their own families. In order to do this, they first cultivated their characters. In order to do this, they first set their hearts right. To set their hearts right, they first made their thoughts sincere. To make their thoughts sincere, they first increased their knowledge to the utmost. To increase their knowledge, they investigated the true nature of all things.

When their knowledge was complete, their thoughts were sincere. When their thoughts were sincere, their hearts were set right. When their hearts were set right, they could cultivate their characters. When they had cultivated their characters, they could regulate their families. When their families were regulated, their states were in good order. When their states were in good order, the whole country was made peaceful and happy.

Confucius taught that the character of the individual is the root of all his actions. When the root is cared for, all that springs from it will be good. He did not live to see his great success and the proof of his teaching; but the future glory of his country was founded on the principles that he so urgently taught.

LAO-TSE

At this same time there lived a man, somewhat older than Confucius, who pointed out the opposite aspect of religion from that which Confucius emphasized. They both believed in the Tao, the Way of Heaven, and that men must live in accord with it; but Lao-tse* made the relation with the Tao all-important and said that if men held fast to that and were true to it, all else would follow, and peace and harmony would reign. He scorned learning, rules, and organization, on which the wise men hitherto had concentrated, and believed in returning to a primitive but spiritual simplicity.

Very little is known about his life. He is supposed to have been born about 600 B.C. and to have served at the royal court as secretary and keeper of the archives. We are not even sure of his name, for the title he is known by means simply "the Old Master." The story goes that in his old age he mounted an ox and rode off into the west and that, when he reached the boundary, the warden begged him to write a book before he disappeared. He did this and left behind him a book of about five thousand characters, much of it in rhymed verses. Then he rode off toward the sunset. Whether this is true or not, it is too good a story to disregard; there are paintings and carvings, in jade and other stones, figures cast in bronze and brass, that show him sitting sideways or astride on his ox, with a scroll in his hand, and it is well to recognize him when one sees him.

A short book remains to us of his sayings, which had a profound influence in China and in other parts of the world. They are very brief, hard to translate and often hard to understand, and yet their gist is clear.[13]

---

*pronounced low (as in now) - dze

Lao-tse riding on a water buffalo. *(Collection of the National Palace Museum, Taipei, Taiwan, Republic of China)*

The way that can be spoken is not the eternal Way;
The name that can be named is not the eternal Name.
Heaven and Earth came from that which cannot be named;
That which is named brought forth the ten thousand things, each after its kind.
Only he who is free from desire can perceive the Inner Essence;
He who is bound by desire sees only the outer appearance.
The inner and the outer come from the same source.
This sameness is the mystery of mysteries, the doorway into all mystery.

This sounds more Indian than Chinese, but people are alike all over the world, and the longing for what is unchanging and eternal belongs to them all, in greater or less degree.

Lao-tse says of the Tao:

The Tao is like an empty vessel that may be drawn from, without its ever needing to be refilled.
It is the base from which Heaven and Earth sprang;
It is there within us all the while.
Draw upon it as you will, it never runs dry.
To it all things owe their existence and it rejects none; yet having produced them it does not take possession of them.
It clothes and nourishes them, but does not claim them; it asks for nothing from them.
They all return to it, still not knowing that it is their master.

Thirty spokes come together to make a wheel;
but it is the nothingness at the center
that makes the wheel useful.

We fashion clay into a pot;
but it is the hollowness within the pot that makes it useful.
We pierce the walls of a house to make doors and windows;
their usefulness depends on the emptiness that they enclose.
Therefore we profit not only by what is, but by what is not.

Try to attain to absolute emptiness; hold fast to perfect stillness.
All things come to flower and fullness and then return to the root from which they grew.
To return to the root is perfect stillness.
In attaining stillness they fulfill their destiny;
In turning back they join the Tao.
To know the Tao is to be enlightened.

One whose life is based on the Tao may go anywhere and never fall a prey to buffalo or tiger;
in battle he need not fear weapons.
For the buffalo would find no place to drive in its horns; the tiger would find no place to thrust its claws, or the weapon its blade.
And why? Because in such a man there is no place of death.

Lao-tse, too, cared about government and believed, as Confucius did, in the power of example:

The Tao never acts, yet through it all things are done.
If princes and kings possessed it, the ten thousand creatures would at once be transformed . . . and so, of itself, the whole country would be at rest.

Now this belief is part of the early tradition; Confucius would have agreed heartily. But Lao-tse is very different in the method that he recommends and in the end that he desires.

> When the Tao is forgotten, we have kindness and justice.
> When knowledge and learning appear, we have hypocrisy.
> When the family no longer lives in harmony, we have filial duty and devoted parents; when the country is torn with strife and disorder, we have loyalty and allegiance. . . .
> Give up your wisdom, discard knowledge, and the people will be a hundred times better off. . . .
> If we do not prize things that are hard to get, there will be no more thieves. If we do not display things that arouse desire, the hearts of the people remain calm and undisturbed.
> Therefore the sage rules by emptying their hearts and filling their stomachs; he weakens their ambitions and strengthens their muscles; he keeps them without knowledge and without desire.
> He governs without action and everything is well regulated.

We shall never know how this sort of government might have worked, for it was never tried. But Lao-tse's words were treasured by many people. Not everyone wanted to live the warm and secure but confined life of the family, and not everyone wanted to serve in the government. There was an adventurous and a vagabond side to the Chinese character, and there were also people who longed for the spiritual experience that can only be had through inner searching and solitary meditation. Such men were encouraged by the sayings of the Old Master and of followers of his; they went off into the beautiful mountains of China or beside rivers and lakes and lived hermits' lives, meditating on the Tao.

It is said of one of them that the prince of a powerful state learned of his wisdom and sent messengers to him, inviting him to become the state's chief minister. "Sirs," was the answer, "have you seen a sacrificial ox? It is fattened with good food and decked with embroidered trappings. But when it is led to slaughter in the temple, would it not gladly change places with any neglected calf? Go away and leave me to enjoy my life in my own way!"

This would have shocked a follower of Confucius. Although the religious beliefs of the two men stemmed from the same root and might have fulfilled each other, Lao-tse providing the spiritual aspect and Confucius the moral and social one, their methods and aims were so different that there were now two teachings instead of one, that of Confucius being always the stronger.

For Lao-tse was true to his own belief and left behind him no rules and no organization at all. "My words are very easy to understand and easy to practice," he said, "but few understand them and few practice them." And few did. But other men, far less wise and far more interested in worldly gain than he was, seized upon his words and used them in ways that he would never have sanctioned. He had said, for example, that the man whose life was based on the Tao need not fear wild animals or weapons of war. This and other statements were made to mean that such a man had supernatural powers of all sorts that enabled him to fly through the air, to heal sickness, to live forever. Magic had a powerful appeal to the Chinese, and the noble religion of Lao-tse became in time one that was mostly concerned with magic, with alchemy, with elixirs that promised immortality. It acquired gods, priests, and temples and was wrongly known as Taoism.

Buddhism, too, although its founder left it highly organized, had been changed and elaborated in ways that would have surprised him. This happens to all religions, because the high and enlightened doctrines of the first teachers must be brought down to the understanding of ordinary people. The difference between the sayings of Lao-tse and the religion that bore his name was very great indeed.

POPULAR BELIEFS

It will be well to say something here about the beliefs of the great majority of the people who were not educated—the many farmers, the skillful artisans, the small merchants, all the people who worked with their hands and provided food and goods for everyone. Both Confucius and Lao-tse, those great and wise men, believed that these people would be quite happy if their lives were secure and comfortable, if they were justly governed and interfered with as little as possible. This was a very enlightened point of view, especially in the fifth and sixth centuries B.C., but it was still not enough.

Although they were an important part of the social structure and observed the Five Relationships, the people had only a small part in the national worship. Only the king could worship Heaven and Earth; only the feudal prince or the city magistrate worshiped the mountains and rivers, the seasons, the soil and the grain. The people made offerings only to their ancestors and to the domestic gods. There was no public worship such as there is in the West, no temples to visit, no priests or monks to teach them. Yet they felt all around them the powers of nature, as their ancestors had done, and they responded to these with sensitive imagination.

They built up a wealth of mythology, of folklore, of fairy tales and ghost stories that would fill more volumes than the Five Classics and the Four Books. To all the spirits of earth and heaven they added goblins and elves and monstrous animals. They also believed in ghosts, for since it was so important to honor and nourish the spirits of one's ancestors, what became of those spirits who had no descendants or whose families neglected or forgot them? They wandered about and worked off their resentment on anyone they could frighten. The ghosts of those who had died tragically were also dangerous: those who had drowned lured people to a watery death; those who had killed themselves tried to make others do so.

One day a man was walking along a road when he was joined by a person dressed in black, who greeted him and said, "Come with me and I will take you to the fairies." He took the man to a lake and showed him, far out on the waters, beautiful palaces and gardens where he could see dancing figures and hear faint music. "Come," said his guide, "let's join them. Just jump into the water!" The credulous man was about to do so when he heard a voice saying, "Stop! A devil is tempting you." He turned and saw his father's spirit, but his black-gowned companion drove it away. The next thing the foolish man knew he was being pulled out of the water by a passerby and then taken home, having learned, let us hope, a salutary lesson.[14]

Certain animals were believed to have magic powers, especially the fox; he was able to live for hundreds of years and to change into human form. Sometimes he was mischievous, sometimes helpful.

A young man was in love with a girl whose family would not allow him to marry her. He was heartbroken and went away to live in another town. One day his sweetheart, with her maid, came to his door. "My family has relented," she said, "and sent me to you." He was overjoyed; they married and were very happy. Shortly afterward a friend from their old home came by; he was amazed to see the young wife. "But she is at home," he said, "still sad and pale, longing for you. I saw her a few days ago."

When the friend returned home, he told the wife's parents what he had seen, and they were so afraid that people might think that their daughter was living illegally with the young man that they decided to marry her to him at once. So they sent for him, and when he came to their house he saw, to his amazement, the girl he thought he had married. He realized that some trick had been played upon him; but he married her nonetheless. When he went to his bride's room after the ceremony, he found two identical lovely maidens smiling at him. One of them came forward and said, "I am a fox. A long time ago your grandfather was out hunting and wounded me by mistake. He took me home and cared for me until I was healed. I have long wanted to repay his kindness, and now I have done it by bringing about your marriage." With that she vanished.[15]

A young scholar was very fond of the bottle; he usually drank a few cups of wine before going to bed and kept an extra bottle beside him in case of need. One night he woke and realized that someone was in bed with him; he reached out and felt a furry body. He lit a lamp and saw a fox, dead drunk and fast asleep beside him, and the extra bottle was empty. "Aha!" he thought. "A kindred spirit!" and went to sleep again. In the morning a charming young man stood beside the bed. "I thank you for sparing my life last night," he said. "We foxes can take a human form by an act of will, but if we get drunk we lose our will power and take our own form again." "Do not thank me," said the young man. "Come as often as you like." The fox did come often and helped the scholar in many ways. Because they live in holes, foxes are believed to know about buried treasure. He showed the young man some hidden money and gave him good advice about some shrewd business deals. The scholar became rich and honored; he married and raised a family and the fox became a household pet.[16]

The Taoist priests traded on these easy beliefs and set themselves up as magicians and wonder-workers. A farmer was selling his pears one day in the market when a ragged priest begged him for one of them. The man refused and drove the priest away; but an onlooker took pity on him and bought him a pear. The priest thanked him and ate it, carefully keeping the seeds. "Now you shall eat some of mine," he said. He planted the seeds then and there in the ground and, to the amazement of a crowd that had gathered, a pear tree grew up before their eyes and was shortly covered with fruit. The priest picked and handed round the pears, which were delicious; then he broke off a branch of the little tree and went away. The farmer who had refused him had drawn near and watched with open mouth; but when he went back to his cart, he found that all his pears had vanished and that one of the handles of his cart had been broken off.[17]

It was not only the uneducated who were deceived by these tricks; several people, even an emperor, died of drinking the elixir of immortality, mixed by the priests.

Though the great ceremonies were performed by the rulers, there were a great many holidays and festivals in the course of the year, in which everyone took part, and these were celebrated all over China until very modern times. Some of them were religious, celebrating the seasons: at the New Year a two-week festival was held, ending with the Feast of Lights, when paper lanterns of every shape, size, and color were hung in the houses and the streets; in the spring the graves of the ancestors were visited and cared for. There was a star festival in July and one for the moon in August. In June there were the Dragon Boat races, in memory of a noble minister of the Chou Dynasty who had drowned himself because his king would not listen to his advice; in autumn there was a day for kite-flying, and this was not only a child's game but often needed all of a man's strength and dexterity. On all these occasions the people showed their skills: plays were acted, music was performed; clever acrobats and jugglers did their tricks; all sorts of toys, lanterns, kites, and tempting foods were sold in the streets.

Tonight I stay at the Summit Temple.
Here I could pluck the stars with my hand;
I dare not speak aloud in the silence,
For fear of disturbing the dwellers in Heaven.
—Li Tai Po

CONFUCIANISM AND BUDDHISM

In 221 B.C. the feudal system destroyed itself, and the Chou Dynasty came to an end. The largest of the states finally conquered all the others, including the small domain of the last kings of Chou. By putting to death all who opposed him, with their families, its ruler reigned over the whole country and called himself the First Great Emperor. He believed that his dynasty would last for a thousand years. It lasted for only fifteen, but in that short time he unified China, put an end to the feudal system, and created an empire which continued into the present century. But he did it with such cruelty and tyranny that the people rose up against him, led by the bold and enterprising headman of a village.

This man established the great Han Dynasty, which lasted from 220 B.C. to A.D. 202. The early emperors of this dynasty, with the advice of wise ministers, wanted to prevent two things from happening again: another time of civil war, like that of the Warring States, or a tyranny like that of the First Emperor. They were wise enough to return to the early tradition of government that Confucius had taught and to base their rule upon the Five Classics and the Four Books.

In order to do this, schools and colleges were built: a great university of six colleges in the capital city and schools in all the provinces and all the towns and districts. There had been schools before this, but everything had been disrupted and disordered during the time of the Warring States, and had to be restored. It was done with extraordinary success. Government posts were given to men who passed examinations in the Classics and who were ranked according to the extent of their knowledge and understanding. Character was equally important; a candidate was not sent up from the provinces to be examined in the capital unless he was a good son and observed the ceremonies. Men flocked to the schools, all over the country, and they were gladly employed, for they were needed.

The feudal princes had been replaced, under the First Great Emperor, by governors whom he appointed and could control, and this system was followed by the Han emperors. The governors must have their cabinets, secretaries, record-keepers, treasurers, and so forth; so must the magistrates of towns and districts. In the Imperial University there were schools of law, mathematics, and calligraphy (the writing, with brush and ink, of the intricate characters). Teachers were needed, and there was work for anyone who could qualify, from the farmer's son to the emperor's son. Nothing, unfortunately, was done for women. Women's minds develop when men's do, and many a woman must have longed for wider fields than the courtyards of the home that she hardly ever left.

The examination system was elaborated and more carefully organized under the Tang Dynasty, a few centuries after the Han. No human institution always lives up to its own highest standards: there were times of laxity and times of corruption, times when learned and virtuous men had to contend with the intrigues of palace eunuchs; but by and large, the examination system gave China a succession of wise and learned ministers, governors, and lesser magistrates and officials. It gave a firm foundation and continuity to the great dynasties: the Tang, the Sung, the Yuan, the Ming, and the Ching, which was the last. Because of the stability and continuity of the government, the splendid arts and industries of the Chinese could flourish and attain a beauty unsurpassed by any other people.

And what, the reader may ask, has this to do with religion? It has everything to do with it. The first of the Five Relationships is that between ruler and subject; the chief concern of the great sages, who were so highly honored, was good government. Harmony in the state and the family was the Way of Heaven; it was man's contribution to the cosmic harmony as well as the source of his happiness. It was a high ideal and a religious one; philosophy does not command such obedience as this.

In the West it is called Confucianism, for it was Confucius who called his people back to their original beliefs and set the Classics before them as the very laws of life. It is not called by this name in China, but is known as the Scholar's Doctrine, or the Teaching of the Sages, a title that would surely have pleased the Master.

It was during the Han Dynasty, when Confucianism was established so firmly as the national religion, that Buddhism was brought to China. It is said that the Emperor Ming Ti, in the year A.D. 67, dreamed that a golden man with a light around his head appeared to him. This vision impressed him so much that he told his courtiers about it and they said that it must be the Indian god Fo-tu, as the name of Buddha was pronounced in Chinese. Buddhism had been heard of before this, but now the Emperor sent envoys into Central Asia to find out about it; it was impossible at that time to go directly into India. The envoys brought back a Buddhist monk who was followed shortly by a second, for the Buddhists were willing missionaries.

These men began the long and difficult work of translating the Indian books into Chinese. The two languages are as different as languages can be, and the work was very hard. But it was done by Indian monks and Chinese converts; more and more Buddhists came into China, mostly from the kingdoms of central Asia which had adopted the Dharma. Later, Chinese pilgrims made the long, dangerous journey into India itself, to see the holy places and to find more books.

For Buddhism took a strong hold on the Chinese. It filled an emptiness left by their own faith and by Confucius himself. Very little had been said about the condition of life after death; the great mass of the people had only their ancestors and their domestic gods to look after them. They had filled this emptiness, as you know, with a host of ghosts and goblins, with fairy tales and myths, but there was much fear in these beliefs, of homeless ghosts and evil spirits who could lure one to a dreadful death.

Buddhism offered, first of all, the definite and logical doctrine of reincarnation, the certainty of survival and the assurance that a happy or a tragic future was in one's own hands; for a good life was rewarded and a bad one punished. Although the first monks who came to China may have been of the Hinayana sect, it was the Mahayana that prevailed. If reincarnation seemed wearisome, there was the Pure Land, the paradise of Amitabha, where one could be reborn if one repeated his name (in China, O-mi-to-fu) often enough, or even once at the point of death.

To the fearful it offered the kindly and gracious Bodhisattvas, whose divine lives were devoted to helping and saving all people. Their lovely images were visible and tangible, and stood before very long in the temples that were built as part of every monastery and were open to all people. The temples usually stood in quiet courtyards paved with wide stones and shaded by great trees. Inside, the light of many lamps flickered in the haze of incense and gleamed on the gilded or painted images, which stood or sat, still and serene, holding in their hands the symbols of blessing or of teaching. The monks chanted to the sound of gongs and cymbals, and the monastery bells were heard over the busy streets or the countryside. There had been no such buildings before.

The most beloved of the Bodhisattvas was Kuan-yin, who was originally an Indian god but who changed his sex in China and became the Goddess of Mercy. This change mattered very little, because in his long spiritual pilgrimage the Bodhisattva had often been born as a woman, and was now, like the angels, beyond the condition of sex. But the Chinese pictured her as a woman and made many images and paintings of her. She would save people from any danger, and women prayed to her for sons. Although prayers had always been offered at sacrifices, there had never been a being in human form to whom anyone could kneel and confide his private sorrows and pray for help.

Another much-loved Bodhisattva (shortened to Pu-sa in China) is Ti-tsang, whose name means, literally, "Earth-Treasury," because he is as firm and trustworthy as the earth and has in his heart a treasure of help and compassion. He is represented as a monk with shaven head, carrying in his right hand a staff whose end is fitted with rings that tinkle as he walks, to warn any small creatures on the path to move away lest they be stepped on. In his left hand he holds a shining jewel. His chief concern is to look after people who have been sent to hell and to free them if possible. Since the Mahayana had offered a paradise, a hell, too, had to be imagined for those who had been wicked and who had not repented and called upon Amitabha. Hell was not everlasting, for everything and everyone was moving toward Buddhahood; it was more like the Western idea of purgatory, for, dreadful as the torments were, when the evil deeds had been expiated, the sufferer was reborn into the world to continue his spiritual journey.

If a man or woman, chastened by the torments he was undergoing, called upon Ti-tsang, he would come, strike open the gates of hell with his staff, flood the darkness with the light of his uplifted jewel, and lead the sinner out to a better life. He was the special protector of children who had died.

These charming figures and their stories were for

A Japanese statue of Ti-tsang, called Jizo in Japan. *(The Metropolitan Museum of Art, Rogers Fund, 1918)*

those who could not understand the higher doctrines of Buddhism, just as the innumerable gods of India are for those who are not yet able to look within themselves for the true Self.

The Chinese added to the many schools of Buddhism a new school, whose name reveals its history. *Dhyana* is the Indian word for meditation; it was changed in China to *Chan* and in Japan to *Zen,* which is now the best-known title of this sect.

Meditation had been known in India from the earliest times, but not in China. The Taoists were the first to go off by themselves and to become hermits. There was much in the Mahayana that was like the true Taoism. Lao-tse had spoken of the Tao as emptiness: "The Tao is like an empty vessel that may be drawn from without ever needing to be refilled." This might have been said by a Mahayanist, whose word for the Infinite was the Void.

Zen was a combination of Buddhism and Taoism and the common sense and humor of the Chinese. They were not so much inclined as the Indians to spend a lifetime, still less many lifetimes, in strenuous mental discipline. Zen is known as the "sudden" school. The Mahayana taught that every living creature possessed the Buddha nature. If so, why strive after it? "Look into your own heart; you are Buddha." The great truth of life must simply be realized, and it can be realized at any moment, if one is able to do so. The Buddha nature is what the Hindus call the Self: it is the Spirit, that which unites all things. It is One.

Therefore, the Zen masters taught, you must never think in relative terms, as if there were two. You cannot seek for enlightenment or long for it, for then there are two: you who seek and that which is sought; you who long and that which is longed for. Seeking enlightenment was called "riding an ox in search of the ox." Books are of no use; speech is of no use; study and knowledge merely hinder you. You must just go about your daily business, eating, working, sleeping, keeping in mind that you and everything in the universe are in truth One. Then suddenly, one day, you will realize it and your whole life will be different. You will still eat, work, and sleep, but your heart will be at peace and your life filled with joy and freedom. You will have awakened.

While books and even words were not valued in the Zen monastery, the teacher was; for realization was an intuitive act and could be transmitted to a disciple from a wise teacher, who knew just when the disciple was ready for it. Often a shock would send the student over the edge, and there are many records of the methods used by Zen teachers to bring their students to awakening.

Zennists claim that the Buddha was the first teacher of their method. One day he was sitting with his disciples at the time when he usually taught them. He had been given a flower; he held it up and said not a word. Most of the monks waited for him to speak; but one of them smiled. It was to this one that the Buddha, when he died, gave his cloak and his begging bowl, thus making him the head of the brotherhood.

The Zen teacher often wanted to shake the students out of their customary channel of thoughts. "Look at that stone," he might say. "Is it inside or outside your mind?" "What was your original face, before you were born?" A satisfactory answer must be found for these riddles, and it was not easily found. Sometimes it was the student who questioned. "How can I be free?" asked one. "Who binds you?" answered the teacher. "No one binds me." "Then why do you want to be free?" and that was enough. Sometimes when a student asked a question, the master merely shouted at him or struck him in order to give him the final shock.

Even the monks could teach one another. One Zen monk went to see another who lived in a lonely hermitage. While they were talking, a tiger growled nearby. The visitor jumped. "I see it is still with you, " remarked the hermit, whose name was Fa-yung. He meant, of course, that the other still feared the animal and felt separate from it. A little later, when his host was absent, the visitor wrote the name of Buddha on the rock where Fa-yung was wont to sit. When Fa-yung came out again, he saw the holy name and hesitated to sit down upon it. "Ah!" said his guest, "I see it is still with you!" and Fa-yung was further awakened.[18]

Although Zen is called the sudden school, it must never be thought that it is a shortcut or an easy way to enlightenment. The teacher does not often administer these shocks to anyone who has not been prepared by years of discipline and meditation. This school and the more "gradual" schools of Buddhism have been compared to the climbing of a steep mountain. One way is to go back and forth on a zigzag, ever-rising path; another is to go straight up to the summit. The short, straight path is not the easier way.

The Zen school and the Pure Land school, which was so very different, became the two most popular Buddhist sects and lasted after the others had declined.

It is too clear and so it is hard to see.
A fool once searched for a fire with a lighted
lantern;
Had he known what fire is,
He could have cooked his rice much sooner.

—*Zen poem*

China, then, from the early centuries had three religions. Confucianism was always the most important, and Buddhism was next. Buddhism was at its height during the great Tang Dynasty; but during the Sung Dynasty (960 to 1280), which followed the Tang, there was a revival of Confucianism led by a group of scholars, the most brilliant being Chu Hsi,* who wrote many books about it. The traditional beliefs had been enriched both by Buddhism and the sayings of Lao-tse. Chu Hsi writes:

> The Great Unity is simply what is highest of all, beyond which nothing can be. It is the most high, most spiritual, most mysterious, surpassing everything . . . In regard to Heaven and Earth, the Great Unity is in Heaven and Earth. In regard to the ten thousand things, it is in them too . . . It is in each individual in its entirety, undivided. It is like the moon, that is not divided although it is reflected in rivers and lakes and is everywhere visible.

The firm foundation of Confucianism, restated by the Sung scholars, brought prosperity and stability to China. Dynasties rose and fell, but there were no more long intervals of disunion like those at the end of the Chou or the Han dynasties. Even when the country was conquered by the Tatars there was no break in the continuity of its culture.

It was during the reign of the Mongol emperor, Kublai Khan, grandson of the terrible Jenghiz, that the Polo brothers of Venice, with young Marco, arrived after a two-year journey across Asia. They could hardly believe

---

*pronounced shee

their eyes as they looked upon the beauty and splendor of China, which at that time far surpassed any other country in the arts of civilization. In his subsequent book, Marco also praises the traditional way of life that he witnessed:

> They bow to each other with cheerful faces and great politeness; they behave like gentlemen and eat very properly. They show great respect for their parents. You hear no feuds or noisy quarrels; in their business dealings they are honest and truthful and there is so much good will and neighborly feeling that you would think that all the people on one street were of the same family. They treat the foreigners who visit them with great cordiality, giving them every help and advice in their business.

ENCOUNTER WITH THE WEST

The encounter of the Eastern nations with the West has been a profoundly disturbing and difficult experience for them and especially for China.

After the Polos returned to Venice, there was a long time when no Europeans appeared in the East. At the end of the fifteenth century the Portuguese made the desperate journey around Africa by sea, in search of trade. They went first to India, but soon discovered the wealth of China and visited its ports, followed by the Dutch and the French. The Europeans had a great advantage over other peoples; they had developed the use of firearms and could defeat anyone who did not use those deadly weapons. The trade with China was so profitable that, during the nineteenth century, more and more Westerners came, although the Chinese tried to keep them out. The foreigners made more and more demands, and when these were refused, they made war. By 1900 China was in danger of being divided among four or five Western nations.

It was not only material force that threatened the whole culture of China; it was also the ideas and accomplishments of the West that invaded and changed it. The facts of science and the power of machinery could not be denied; the ideas of democracy and of individual freedom were also new and exciting. There were men in China who eagerly accepted these new ways of living and who realized that their country must adapt itself to great changes or else be conquered. Unfortunately, an old and dying dynasty was still in power; it was headed by an ignorant and headstrong woman, the Empress Dowager, who opposed all change and was able to put to death or to banish all who favored it.

The dynasty was overthrown in 1911 by a revolution led by Sun Yat-sen, who was so far influenced by Western ideas that he tried to set up a republic, instead of a new dynasty. This was impossible in a country that had been an empire for four or five thousand years and was already deeply upset and poor as a result of foreign wars. China was in turmoil for the next forty years.

Some of the men who were trying to save their country had gone to Europe and America and had read widely about different theories of government, including Communism. The empire had failed; the republic had failed. They believed that only Communism, with its stern discipline, its ruthless methods, its intense industrialization, and its centralized power, could cope with the desperate condition their people were in. They set themselves up against the republicans, and civil war followed. The Communists won in 1949 and have been in power ever since.

This victory brought to an end the traditional religion

and culture of China. Already, before the revolution of 1911, Western ideas were undermining the family system. Young people wanted their own homes when they married; young men and women wanted to choose whom they should marry and what work they would do. The family was the very foundation of society, and when it crumbled, much else fell with it. The old system of government was abandoned in 1911. These were the two strong pillars of Confucianism. Communism speeded the overthrow of the old beliefs. Communists care very much for the welfare of the people, but they believe that it can be accomplished best by scientific methods and human effort; they discourage all religious belief. They have brought unity and increased prosperity to China and have restored its pride and power. But the religion of Confucius and the culture which it created have come to an end. A century is a short time in China's history; the fraction of a century still less. No one knows what remains of their long and rich tradition in the hearts and minds of the people; no one knows what may happen in the future.

There remains in Peking, as evidence of the former faith, one of the most beautiful places of worship in the world, the Altar of Heaven. It is a series of three concentric, circular terraces of white marble, each one surrounded with a balustrade of the same stone. It is wide open to the sky, like the first simple altar raised by the mythical emperor, Fu Hi. Each terrace has four flights of nine steps, leading from the north, south, east, and west. Each stone is laid with meaning and purpose; the topmost terrace is paved with nine circles of marble stones which form multiples of nine, the outermost circle having eighty-one stones. The altar is surrounded by a low circular wall, pierced at each of the four cardinal points by three marble

The Altar of Heaven, in Peking. *(Dimitri Kessel: Life Magazine © 1955 Time, Inc.)*

Detail of the Altar of Heaven. *(The Bettmann Archive, Inc.)*

gates. Beyond this is a square wall with similar gates, and the whole is embedded in a great park of fine old trees.

Here, in the cold, dark hours before the dawn of the winter solstice, the reigning emperor came to make his offerings to Heaven, to his immediate ancestors, and to the powers of the visible heaven: the sun, moon, and planets, the rain and wind and clouds. There were no symbols of deity except the tall tablets inscribed with the names of each one. These were placed on the topmost terrace, and there the emperor prostrated himself, giving thanks for the blessings of the past year and praying for the coming one. If he was a worthy ruler, he interceded for all the people, taking their sins upon himself, for he was the One Man, the mediator between Heaven and man. His ministers stood, each in his place, on the lower terraces, and the scene was lighted by great lanterns of translucent horn.

Just north of the altar is a small temple where the sacred tablets and other implements of ceremony were kept. Beyond that, at the end of a wide, straight avenue, is the beautiful building usually called the Temple of Heaven, but more correctly the Temple of Prayer for the Year, where, in the spring, the emperor prayed for a fruitful and happy year. It stands upon three tiers of marble terraces and has three roofs of blue tiles that rise above the surrounding trees.

The whole compound is magnificently simple and beautiful, for it was laid out in accord with the deepest conviction and purpose of the people of China: to live, in every detail of life, in harmony with the Way of Heaven.

In the spring
The foliage of the willow tree
Sweeps down like long strands of hair.
In summer, the moon
Shines more softly in the sky.
In autumn the flowers of the cinnamon tree
Are white.
In winter, we recite poetry
Around the lamp.
I am very satisfied to be alive.
Sometimes, looking at a stone
Or listening to the wind
Contents me.

—*Chang Kyu Ling*

Izanami and Izanagi create the world. *(Courtesy, Museum of Fine Arts, Boston)*

PART FIVE

Shinto, the Way of the Gods

The beaten path
Is covered with fallen leaves;
Brush them aside and see
The footprints of the Sun Goddess.

—*Ninomiya*

The Japanese people have believed from the beginning of their history to the present day that their beautiful islands are the land of the gods, the first land to be created out of the vast expanse of ocean. After the islands were formed, all created things, including man and a multitude of gods, were born there. For this reason the people have a spiritual kinship with mountains and rivers, rocks and trees, and with all living creatures; for there is no dividing line between them: the only difference is in the degree of consciousness or in the particular part that each one plays in the working of the whole. The islands, in all their aspects, and all those who are born there are of one family and the head of this family is the emperor, for they believe that he is the direct and biological descendant of the greatest of all the deities, the Sun Goddess.

When one makes such a statement about the people of any country it must be remembered that it is a generalization, that there are many individuals who believe differently and others who do not believe anything at all. Nonetheless, when people form a community that lasts for hundreds or for thousands of years and when the vast majority of them hold certain beliefs and live by them, it seems justifiable. The religion of the Japanese is called Shinto, and it has been the most powerful influence in their lives.

Shinto originated in the very early days of their history and is therefore expressed in mythical stories, as almost all early beliefs are. The Japanese mythology is rich and detailed and it is still a vital part of the national life.[1]

This is their story of creation:

In the beginning, when heaven and earth began, certain great powers came into being. They were given names, and in a large, vague way, personalities; they symbolized the first movements of creativity and growth. There were six generations of these divine beings, and the seventh produced two much more definite figures: one male, whose name was Izanagi; and one female, Izanami. They were sent down from the High Plain of Heaven by the older gods to create the world.

They stepped out upon the Floating Bridge of Heaven and looked downward. Izanagi said, "Is there not something beneath us?" He thrust down his jeweled spear and found the ocean. When he pulled the spear out, some brine dripped from it and formed an island. They stepped down upon it and lived there.

They built a house for themselves with a central pillar, and when it was done, Izanagi said, "Let us go round the heavenly central pillar, and when we meet at the other side, let us be united in wedlock and give birth to other lands." So they walked round, she to the right, he to the left, and when they met, she said, "How delightful! I have met a lovely youth!" And he said, "How delightful! I have met a lovely maiden!" But then he was angry and said to her, "You should not have spoken first, for you are a woman." For this reason, probably, their first child was ill-formed, and they put him in a reed boat and set him adrift upon the ocean.

Meanwhile, they had gone round the pillar again, and Izanagi had spoken first. They gave birth to the other islands of Japan. They also bore a multitude of gods, some born in the usual way and others in strange ways from almost any part of their bodies. Spirits of rocks, of trees, of winds and waters, of mountains and valleys, of grasses and herbs, appeared. Finally Izanami brought forth the God of Fire, and in doing so, was so badly burned that she died and went to the land of Yomi, or darkness.

Izanagi was so angry with the fire-child that he cut him into three pieces, and eight gods were born of the blood that dripped from his sword. Then he sought his beloved wife in the land of darkness. Izanami came out to meet him. "My lovely younger sister," said he, "the lands that you and I made are not yet finished; so come back!"

"Why did you not come sooner, my lord and husband?" answered his wife. "I have already eaten of the food of Yomi and cannot return. But I will discuss it with the lord of Yomi. Do not look at me!" She went into the lord's palace; but she lingered so long that Izanagi broke off the end-tooth of the comb that he wore in his hair, lighted it for a torch, and went to look for her. When he found her, he saw that her body was already decayed and loathsome and he turned and fled. She was very angry and cried out, "Why did you not obey me? Now you have put me to shame!" She sent the Ugly Women of Yomi to chase him and slay him, and she joined them. He threw down his comb, which changed into bamboo sprouts, and the Ugly Women pulled them up and ate them, and then took up the pursuit again. He threw down his headdress, which turned into bunches of grapes, and again his pursuers stopped to eat them, and he escaped.

When he reached the mouth of the underworld, he rolled a great rock against it and stopped it up. Just then Izanami caught up with him, and from the other side of the rock he said, "Our marriage is ended." "If you divorce me," she answered, "I will kill a thousand of the people of your land in one day." "If you do so," he said, "I will in one day cause fifteen hundred to be born." And these angry words were the last they spoke to each other.

When Izanagi regained the upper world, he said to himself, "I have been in a hideous, unclean land. I must purify myself," and he went to the sea and bathed himself thoroughly. As he washed his left eye, the Sun Goddess was born; as he washed his right eye, the Moon God appeared. The Storm God was born from the washing of his nose; his name is Susa-no-wo-no-mikoto and it means Swift-Impetuous-August-Male-Deity. Izanagi was pleased with these three children. The Sun Goddess was such a radiant and glorious creature that he sent her up to take charge of the High Plain of Heaven. Her name is Amaterasu-O-mi-kami, which means "Heaven-Shining-Great-August-Deity."

[Japanese is a hard language for a foreigner to learn, but it is not hard to pronounce the proper names to oneself and therefore to recognize them. Almost every syllable is made up of one consonant and one vowel: sometimes a single vowel makes a syllable, as in I-za-na-gi; sometimes two vowels make one sound, as in *ai* or *ei. G* is always hard, as in go. If one remembers how the vowels are pronounced and divides the syllables the reading is easy, however long the name may be. There is no accent; all syllables have the same value. It is important to know some of these names, and they have a fine rhythm. The "O-mi-kami" and "O-mi-koto" mean "Great-August-Deity" and may be left out.]

Izanagi gave the Moon God the realm of the night, and said to Susa-no-wo, "You shall rule the ocean." But this god was a troublemaker; he would not rule the seas but wept and wailed continually, till the green mountains were washed bare and the rivers ran dry. His father asked him why he wept so much, and he said that he wanted to go to his mother in the underworld. "Then go, as your heart bids you," said Izanagi, glad to be rid of him.

Before Susa-no-wo departed, he went up to the High Plain of Heaven to say good-bye to his sister the Sun Goddess. She knew his character and came out to meet him, armed with a bow and sword. They stood on either side of the River of Heaven (the Milky Way) and as they talked, eight gods were born of their breath. Susa-no-wo convinced his sister that his intentions were pure, and she let him pass, but once he came into her domain, he behaved worse than ever. He broke down the dikes between her rice fields and let the piebald colts of Heaven loose in them; he threw filth into her palace. Finally—worst and strangest of all his misdeeds—while she was sitting in her weaving hall with her maidens, making garments for the gods, he skinned one of the piebald colts and flung it down into the hall through a hole in the roof.

This was too much for his sister. She entered the rock cave of Heaven, closed the door, and left the heavens and the earth in darkness. The gods were horrified. On earth the descendants of Izanagi and the people they ruled over woke in the morning to black night instead of the warm and blessed rays of the sun. The myriads of gods and goddesses met together on the bank of the River of Heaven and took counsel. They uprooted an evergreen tree and set it up beside the cave. From its topmost branches they hung a string of jewels, from the center branches they hung a large mirror of polished metal, and from the lower ones, lengths of soft cloth, blue and white. They brought cocks with them which they set to crowing. Then they all gathered outside the cave.

A gay and mischievous goddess kindled a fire; she turned a tub upside down and danced a rather indecent dance on it, drumming upon it with her feet. The gods shouted with laughter. Ama-terasu, inside the cave, thought to herself, "There must be darkness everywhere without. How can they be so merry?" She went to the mouth of the cave and asked them why they were having such a good time.

"There is someone here more beautiful than you," answered the dancing goddess. Ama-terasu, of course, opened the door a crack, and the first thing she saw was her own radiant reflection in the mirror. The God of Strength, who stood close to the cave, seized her hand, pulled the door wide open, and led her forth. Another one drew a rope of rice straw across the opening, so that she could never go back, and all was well.

Susa-no-wo was punished and expelled from Heaven. Again he did not go right away to the underworld, but descended to earth, to the province of Izumo, on the northwestern shore of the island of Honshu. There he met a man and a woman leading a young girl between them, and all were weeping. He asked why they sorrowed. "I had eight daughters," answered the man. "But every year a great serpent comes and devours one of them. This is our last daughter, and this is the time when the serpent comes. It has eight heads and eight tails and is a very fearful beast." Susa-no-wo told them to prepare eight tubs filled with rice wine; he set these out in a row, and when the serpent came, it put each of its eight heads into a tub and drank until it lay in a drunken stupor. Then he cut the heads off, one by one. In the monster's body he found a great sharp sword which he thought so fine that he gave it to Ama-terasu as a propitiatory gift. He married the girl he had rescued and begot many children, but finally took himself off to the land of Yomi and we hear no more of him. His descendants, as well as other gods who were born of Izanagi and Izanami and lived on the islands, are known as the Earthly Kami, while those who dwelt on the High Plain of Heaven are the Heavenly Kami.

Kami is a word that is hard to define; even the Japanese have difficulty doing so. It is usually translated "god," since we have no equivalent for it in English. Yet Kami does not mean god in the Western sense of the word. We think of gods as persons, separate from and above human beings. There is no dividing line between Kami and any living creature; there is only a succession, a great stream, one might say, of created beings, from the highest and oldest of heavenly powers to the sands of the seashore or the herbs of the field. Kami means, literally, high or superior, and any creature may become a Kami if it possesses the superior qualities that make it worthy of reverence and remembrance. Those great beings who made heaven and earth were, of course, Kami. On the other hand, men and women may become Kami, because of some great virtue, as with us they may become saints. In Japan there is one word for the whole spiritual succession; mountains may be Kami, so may great rocks or trees or rivers. Therefore the word will be used where there is no English equivalent for it.

The Heavenly Kami were not pleased to have these precious islands in the hands of Susa-no-wo's descendants, though the latter had become very worthy people, not at all like their obstreperous ancestor. So they decided to send down Ama-terasu's grandson to rule the earth. They first sent one of the gods to see how things stood. He went out upon the Floating Bridge of Heaven and looked down; then he returned and said that the land was full of evil deities that shone like fireflies and buzzed like summer insects; even the rocks, the trees, and the grasses had voices. It was an unruly land and he would have none of it. Then the gods sent another messenger who never returned. They sent down still another; this one married a daughter of the ruler of the land and wanted it for himself, and for eight years they did not hear from him.

After these experiences it seemed safer to send two envoys. These went directly to the ruler (one of Susa-no-wo's descendants) and asked him if he would yield the country to the grandson of the Sun Goddess. He rather naturally demurred. They made him a more tactful and gracious proposal: that he share the rule with his distant cousin, keeping the spiritual and ceremonial duties in his own hands and yielding the political and military ones to the newcomer. They offered also to build him a beautiful palace. He agreed to this. They expelled the unruly gods and put to silence the herbs, trees, and rocks that formerly had voices, and returned to Heaven to make their report.

Then Ama-terasu-O-mi-kami summoned her grandson, Ninigi-no-mikoto, and said to him, "This land of the Plentiful Reed Plains of Fifteen Thousand Autumns and of Fresh Rice Ears shall be ruled over by my descendants.

Proceed thither, my noble grandson, and govern it. Go! and may prosperity attend your dynasty and may it, like heaven and earth, endure forever!" She named five companions to go with him, and finally she gave him the mirror and the string of jewels that had lured her from the rock cave, and the sword that Susa-no-wo had found in the serpent's body and had given to her. "Think of this mirror as my spirit," she said. "Worship it as you would my very presence."

The August Grandchild, Ninigi-no-mikoto, left the heavenly rock seat with his five companions; "thrusting apart the myriad-piled clouds of Heaven, he clove his way with an awful way-cleaving" and landed on a mountain in the westernmost island which is now called Kyushu. From there he explored the country and found a place that suited him. He built a palace, setting its pillars firmly on the rock and raising its crossbeams to the heavens, and there he dwelt and ruled over the island.

There is no mention in these legends of the creation of man, for in Shinto man is not all-important and he is not the lord of creation. He came into being with all the other creatures and shares the Kami-nature as they all do. There were "people" in Izanagi's time, so there must have been men in the islands under Ninigi's rule. The Heavenly Kami intermarried with them, and their descendants became the inhabitants of the country.

There are many delightful stories about Ninigi, his marriage, and his children; one is especially important. One of Ninigi's sons lost his elder brother's fishhook; he could not find it anywhere. In despair he sat lamenting by the seashore, for his brother was stern and unforgiving. An old man came to him and said, "Do not grieve. Enter the sea and you will find a road that will lead you to the Sea God's palace. Outside the gate is a well, and beside the well, a wide-branching cassia tree. Climb into this tree, and the Sea God's daughter will find you there." The young prince obeyed, and soon the princess came to the well, saw him in the tree, and was astonished by his beauty. She told her father that a stranger was at the gate; he invited Ninigi's son to his palace, feasted him, and eventually gave him his daughter in marriage.

They lived happily there, and a boy was born to them. But after three years the prince became homesick for the earth and for his family. He could not go back without the lost fishhook. The Sea God summoned all the fishes of the ocean and asked them if they had seen it; it was found at last in a fish that had suffered for some time with a sore throat. So the young prince returned home, taking his sea-born son with him.

The son of this child became the first legendary emperor of Japan. His name was Jimmu; he left Kyushu and took possession of the western part of the great island of Honshu, where most of the early history of Japan occurred. There he married a descendant of Susa-no-wo, and so he united in his person the land and the ocean and the families of the Sun Goddess and her brother, the Heavenly and the Earthly Kami. He is believed to be the founder of the empire, and his date is 660 B.C. though the date, like the man, is legendary. He and his descendants ruled over the central part of Honshu, gradually increasing their territory to include the whole island. The people prospered; they built towns and villages, planted the valleys with rice and vegetables, while the rivers and shores gave them an abundance of fish.

The present emperor is the direct descendant of the Emperor Jimmu, therefore of Ninigi-no-mikoto and therefore of Ama-terasu-O-mi-kami. There has been no break in the line of descent; every emperor has been a member of the one family. The Japanese are very proud of this fact because it fulfills the words of the Sun Goddess to her grandson, ". . . may it [your dynasty], like heaven and earth, endure forever!" For this reason he is unique in Japan (the imperial family has no surname, for it needs none) and unique among the rulers of the world. It is believed that when he is enthroned (and not until then) he comes into direct communication with his august ancestors, including Ama-terasu-O-mi-kami, and that they work their will through him. As a Western scholar has said, ". . . the sovereign unites as a whole the Japanese people . . . not only . . . as inhabitants of the Japanese nation, but also in their spiritual relationship with Heaven."[2] The great majority of the people, to this day, look up to their emperor with reverence and devotion and are willing at any moment to lay down their lives for him.

His role is not an easy one. If he is a worthy ruler, he keeps his mind and heart pure and disciplined in order to be an instrument for these higher powers. In addition to all his duties as a constitutional monarch, he is the high priest of the nation and conducts the great ceremonies of the year. His position is very like that of the Chinese ideal: he is the One Man, the Son of Heaven, mediator between Heaven and his people.

There are no sacred scriptures in Shinto, like those of India or China; there are the legends, early chronicles, poems, and ritual. The teaching is mostly traditional. The word Shinto is a Chinese one and means "the Way of the Gods"; in Japanese it is *Kami-no-michi,* which says the same thing. The teaching and the purpose are that everyone shall live in accord with the will of the gods. There are no written commandments, for none are needed. Everyone is born of the gods and possesses the same spiritual nature; therefore one needs only to listen to his own heart and conscience and live as they direct. Purity, uprightness, and sincerity are Shinto virtues; simplicity and cleanliness are outward signs of them.

The first shrines were simple, small buildings of smooth, unpainted wood where the Kami could come to receive offerings and worship. No image was made of them, but symbols that represented their spirits were kept in the inner recesses of the buildings. Sometimes there was a mirror or a stone, a sword or even a cushion, for the Japanese sit on cushions on the floor, and it denoted that the Kami was present. The shrine itself was too small for public worship; people came to it, bowed, and made their offering. Soon larger buildings were raised nearby for public ceremonies, religious dances, and plays, for the shrine was usually set in an enclosure that had room for several buildings and for fine trees. Festivals were held at the time of the rice planting and the harvest, the time of thanksgiving in November, at the New Year and other occasions.

Prayers that were spoken at such times by the priests have come down to us; they are called *norito,* and many of them were written centuries ago. The following is one that was spoken in the emperor's palace.

The priest first addresses all the myriad Kami:

> I humbly declare in the presence of the sovereign gods whose praises are fulfilled as Heavenly Kami and as Earthly Kami:
>
> In the second month of this year the Sovran Grandchild [the emperor] is graciously pleased to pray for harvest and I, therefore, as the morning sun rises in glory, offer up his plenteous offerings . . . of ears a thousand, of ears many a hundred, raising up the tops of the saké-jars and setting in rows the bellies of the saké-jars, in juice and in ear will I present

The Shrine of the Sun Goddess at Ise. The shrine is the tallest of the buildings. *(Japan National Tourist Organization)*

them; of things growing in the great moor-plain, sweet herbs and bitter herbs; of things that dwell in the blue sea-plain, the broad of fin and the narrow of fin, edible seaweed from the offing and from the shore; of clothing, bright stuffs and shining stuffs, soft stuffs and coarse stuffs. With these I will fulfill your praises.

Then he addresses the gods who protect the palace:

Whereas on the nethermost rock-roots the palace pillars have been raised stout and high and the projecting crossbeams exalted to the High Plain of Heaven, furnishing a fair abode for the Sovran Grandchild, wherein, finding shelter from the rain and shelter from the sun, he serenely governs in peace the world on all sides, I fulfill your praises by making these plenteous offerings on his behalf.

Whereas you guard the gates and the four quarters by night and by day, obstructing the passage like manifold piles of rock . . . and guard below against unfriendly things coming from below and guard above against unfriendly things coming from above, I fulfill your praises by making these offerings.

Finally he speaks to the Sun Goddess:

More especially do I humbly declare in the mighty presence of the Great-Heaven-Shining-Deity who dwells in Ise. Because the Great Deity has bestowed on him the lands of the four quarters over which her glance extends as far as where the wall of Heaven rises; as far as where the bounds of earth stand up; as far as the blue clouds are diffused; as far as where the white clouds settle down opposite; by the blue sea-plain, as far as the ships can go without letting dry their poles and oars; by land, as far as the hoofs of horses can go, with tightened baggage-cords, treading their way among rock-roots and tree-roots where the long road extends . . . therefore will the first fruits for the Sovran Great Deity be piled up in her mighty presence like a range of hills, leaving the remainder for him [the emperor] tranquilly to partake of.

Moreover, whereas you bless the Sovran Grandchild's reign as a long reign, firm and enduring, and render it a happy and prosperous reign, I bow my head in reverence to you as our Sovran's dear, divine ancestor and fulfill your praises by making these plenteous offerings in his behalf.[3]

One of the most important festivals was that of Purification, which was celebrated twice a year, in midsummer and at the end of the year. It was called the O-harai. It was performed by the emperor and also throughout the country, and by it all sins, committed knowingly or unknowingly, were washed away and annulled.

Part of the norito read on the occasion is this:

Let him recite the mighty words of the celestial ritual. When he does so, the Gods of Heaven, thrusting open the adamantine door of Heaven and cleaving the many-piled clouds with an awful way-cleaving, will lend ear. The Gods of Earth, climbing to the tops of the high mountains, to the tops of the low mountains, sweeping apart the mists of the high mountains and the mists of the low mountains, will lend ear.

When they have thus lent ear, all offenses whatsoever will be annulled, from the court of the Sovran

> Grandchild to the provinces of the four quarters Under-Heaven.
>
> The goddess who dwells in the rapids of the swift stream whose cataracts tumble headlong from the tops of the high mountains will bear them into the great sea-plain. Thereupon the goddess who dwells in the myriad meetings of the tides of the myriad brine-paths of the myriad ways of the currents of the boisterous sea will swallow them up. Then the goddess who dwells in the Root country, the Bottom country, will banish and abolish them.[4]

At first reading, this mythology seems to be like any other, as delightful as many mythologies are, but now, like most of the others, a thing of the past. This is not true of Shinto. It has lasted into modern times and has still kept the intimate and early communion with the visible universe and its invisible forces. To many people the legendary Kami have become symbols—of benevolence and watchfulness, of purity and creative power. But to many more they are still individual presences and are honored in hundreds and thousands of shrines, great and small, throughout the country. Their names are remembered; their stories are dramatized and danced. Shinto individualizes in innumerable Kami the spiritual presence and power that all religions recognize. In addition to the spirits of nature, each village and town has its local deity, called the Uji-gami. At this shrine every child is presented when it is a month old; there offerings of food are made each day and festivals are held at the important times of the year. Each craft has its guardian Kami; each house, its guardians of the gate, the well, the courtyard, and the kitchen. In the shrines of the imperial palace the same ceremonies are performed; and the symbols of office of the emperor, like the crown and scepter of European kings, are the mirror and the jewels that were offered to Amaterasu in her cave, and the sword that Susa-no-wo found in the serpent's body and gave to her.

CONFUCIANISM AND BUDDHISM COME TO JAPAN

More will be said later about the present practice of Shinto. But now we must turn to its history; for religions have their history, as all human institutions do, and they are tested by it, as people are by their lives. Shinto was tested by close association with Confucianism and Buddhism, and finally by the challenge of the West.

Japan is a young country compared to China and to India. Before it had a written language, it came into contact with China, whose civilization was already more than two thousand years old. It is first mentioned by the Chinese during the Han Dynasty (220 B.C. to A.D. 206) when the Chinese conquered and colonized north and central Korea, which is within easy reach of the island of Kyushu. From that time on, the powerful influence of China seeped into Japan. In A.D. 57 a Japanese mission was received at the court of the Han emperor; the envoys were amazed at the splendor that they saw: the arts and fine buildings, the apparently stable and peaceful government. The Chinese, on the other hand, reported that the people of the islands in the eastern sea were living in a very primitive way, and could not read or write. The younger country was quick and eager to learn; Chinese and Korean scholars, artists and workmen, were invited to come to it, and more and more Japanese went to Korea and then to China to learn.

There, of course, they encountered Confucianism and realized that it was the foundation of all that they admired. They did not need its purely religious aspects, for they had their own Kami and would not change their "dear, divine ancestor," the Sun Goddess, for the more distant and abstract idea of Heaven. They, too, honored the powers of nature and had their own ceremonies. But the Way of Heaven was like their own Way of the Gods; they understood it, and those who went to China were much impressed by the order and beauty of its culture. The Five Relationships they took to heart and based their own social life upon them. For they had a strong feeling for family life and for their ancestry, especially those who claimed direct descent from the many Kami. After they learned the Chinese script they, too, put the "spirit tablets," with the names of their forebears, on a special shelf in the house and offered food each day and lighted a guardian lamp at night. Good manners were inseparable from the Five Relationships, as they were from Shinto; the Japanese became as self-controlled, as ceremonious, and as courteous as their teachers on the continent.

They did not take the first relationship—that between ruler and subject—so seriously. In Confucianism one of the first duties of a ruler was to choose wise and able ministers and governors, who might belong to any social class. This the Japanese did not wholly accept, for their society was aristocratic. Besides, the warrior, not the scholar, came first in the social scale; after him came the farmer, the artisan, and the merchant. Japan was already a feudal country; the emperor was always revered, but the land and the power were in the hands of the great nobles. Feudalism remained there until 1868 whereas in China it ended in 221 B.C.

Buddhism came by the same route, but later. In the year 552, tradition says, the ruler of one of the Korean kingdoms, allied with Japan, sent to the emperor a gilded image of the Buddha, together with some learned men and some Buddhist monks. The new doctrine was welcomed gladly and spread with extraordinary speed and thoroughness. In the seventh century it was ordered that in every Japanese house there should be a Buddhist altar and that food and worship be offered there. Not long after that another order stated that every province should be given a sixteen-foot image of the Buddha; monasteries and nunneries and seven-storied pagodas must also be built. Emperors and nobles vied with one another in rich gifts of land, buildings, images, bells, and gongs. The form of Buddhism that came into Japan was the Mahayana, filtered through China.

Buddhism brought much to Japan. Shinto is mostly concerned with earthly life; it does not look beyond into what may happen after death, and it does not imagine any higher state of consciousness than that of a happy life in this world. Buddhism brought the idea of reincarnation and karma, and the easier doctrine of Amitabha (Amida in Japan) and the Pure Land. It offered the possibility of enlightenment and the vision of the peace and bliss of nirvana, which surpasses all earthly consciousness. It brought its great and voluminous literature and its arts, which inspired those of Japan. Like Confucianism, it was a far more highly developed religion than Shinto had had time to be. The keen minds of the Japanese delighted in its philosophy, its doctrines, and the beauty of the images and architecture that it brought from China. They added their own delicacy and grace to the Chinese models as they carved the lovely images of Buddhas and Bodhisattvas. One of the most beautiful statues in the world is that of the Buddha who is yet to come, who is now a Bodhisattva. It was carved out of wood in the seventh century and is now in a small building on the grounds of the Horiuji temple in Nara. The gleam of lamplight upon these figures, the incense, the chanting of the monks, gave them something quite different from the simplicity of the Shinto shrines.

The Buddha who is yet to come, at the temple of Horiuji in Nara.

In the twelfth century a Japanese monk brought Zen Buddhism from China. It was very congenial to his countrymen: the belief that the Buddha-nature (like the Kami-nature) is in all creatures and that it can be realized in a flash of intuition, the discipline and simplicity of the monks' lives, had an immediate appeal. Zen flourished and developed in Japan, which is now the world center for the study and practice of that teaching.

The followers of the Buddha have adapted their teaching to the needs and the natures of the people of different lands. Since the Dharma had spread over the greater part of Asia, it had to meet other creeds, and if any of them were too strong to do away with, the Buddhists included them in their own doctrine. The monks knew that Shinto was too strong to give way completely to the new faith, so they met it halfway. The chief Shinto gods were said to be manifestations of former Buddhas; Amaterasu was identified with an important Buddha who was originally a sort of Sun God.

The result of this policy was an adjustment between the two religions, which was called Two-fold or Double Shinto. Buddhist priests moved into the Shinto shrines, bringing their images, their rites and music; they took part in the many festivals, side by side with the Shinto priests. Funeral services were not held in the shrines because of the general dislike and horror of death. The Buddhists took charge of all such things, including services and intercession for the spirits of the dead. Shinto shrines became larger and more elaborate; temples dedicated to the two faiths often stood side by side, and it was hard to tell the difference between them. But Shinto was always the more universal and the stronger of the two because it embraced the whole land and all the people; every child was born into it. And the emperors, although some of them were devout Buddhists, never forgot their divine ancestry or ceased to honor Ama-terasu. In spite of their great influence, Buddhists were always a minority.

The great path has no gates;
Thousands of roads enter it.
When one passes through this gateless barrier
He walks freely between heaven and earth.
—Zen poem

FIRST ENCOUNTER WITH THE WEST

At about the time that Zen was brought into Japan, a change took place in the government, which must be noted because of its bearing on later events. The emperor had gradually become a figurehead, a sacred person living in the charming city of Kyoto, mainly concerned with religious ceremony, both Shinto and Buddhist.

The powerful nobles fought each other for land and power. At the end of the twelfth century one family, the Minamoto, fought its way to the top; its leader called himself shogun, or generalissimo, and took over the government, always in the emperor's name. From that time until 1868, the country was ruled—sometimes well and sometimes ill—by shoguns, and the emperors reigned but were powerless. Japan was still feudal: it was divided into territories, some as large as provinces, some small, owned by the nobles, who were called daimyo.* Each of them had an army of warriors, or samurai. It was a strong shogun who could keep them all in order. There was continual fighting which at times amounted to civil war.

It was during a time of turbulence, in 1542, that the first adventurous Portuguese ships arrived in Japan. Others followed and Jesuit missionaries, led by Saint

---

*pronounced dime-yo

Francis Xavier, came with them. The Japanese welcomed these people cordially, glad to trade with them and always eager to hear a new doctrine. Christianity did not seem strange: the Jesuits preached salvation by faith, as the Amidists did; their ritual was very like that in the Buddhist temples, and the images of the Madonna were like those of Kwanyin. They made many converts and built churches. Spanish and Dutch merchants followed the Portuguese, and trade was lively. It went on for nearly a hundred years.

Gradually, however, the shoguns began to distrust the foreigners. The European merchants were competing fiercely for the rich Eastern trade and told terrifying stories about each other. The indiscreet pilot of a Spanish ship told Japanese officials, "Our kings begin by sending missionaries to the countries they wish to conquer. They induce the people to embrace our religion; then troops are sent who combine with the new Christians and our kings have little trouble in accomplishing the rest." The Christian priests made a point of converting the daimyo, for then all the people on the feudal lands could be ordered to change their faith whether they wanted to or not. The shoguns saw that the foreigners were, indeed, beginning to take possession of the countries they traded with.

Meanwhile an extraordinary man became shogun in 1603; his family name was Tokugawa. He was a mighty warrior and, in addition, a great statesman. He organized the government so firmly and so cleverly, with such detailed regulations, that the country remained at peace for two hundred and fifty years under the rule of his descendants. He made Yedo—the present Tokyo—his military capital.

The third Tokugawa shogun, in the 1630's, made a momentous decision. He expelled all foreigners from Japan, and forbade any Japanese to leave the country. No ship could be built large enough to leave the shore for any distance. The Christians had been cruelly persecuted for many years; now there were almost none left. Japan was shut off from the rest of the world; only the Dutch, who had made no trouble, and a few Chinese were allowed to come once a year to the tiny island of Deshima in the bay of Nagasaki. They could not leave it except to make a formal visit to the shogun, to present gifts. This was a most extraordinary decision for a nation to make; Japan lived completely apart from the rest of the world for two hundred and fifteen years.

The long years of peace gave men time for thought. The Tokugawa shoguns and their ministers wanted order, stability, and loyalty, and for those things they turned to the Chinese Classics. But scholars also began to be interested in the history and the religion of their own country. A great daimyo, grandson of the first shogun, collected many books, assembled scholars at his court, and compiled the first history of Japan, in many volumes. Learned men, monks, and Shinto priests looked into the tales of the gods, the early poems and chronicles, the norito and the ceremonies, and found great beauty and value in them.

During the eighteenth century and well into the nineteenth, a succession of scholars revived the early Shinto literature and wrote in praise of it. It was collected and organized into a body of scripture that could stand beside the Chinese and Indian books. They deplored the adoption of Confucianism and Buddhism, forgetting what both had done for the development of their country. Many daimyo and samurai, who had no fighting to do, turned to learning and to the arts. Shinto roused their pride and turned the attention of the samurai beyond their feudal lords to the country and to the emperor. It was his ancestor who had been sent down from Heaven to rule the land. Was it not he who should be ruling it? Many of them resented the power of the shogun who, after all, was one of themselves.

During these centuries of seclusion much had been happening in the rest of the world. While the East was concerned with its arts and philosophies, the West had accomplished wonders with science and technology. The European nations were conquering more and more of Asia with the power of their firearms. Foreign vessels came into Japanese ports, asking for trade, but they were turned away. Russian and American vessels passed within sight of land.

Finally, in July, 1853, a fleet of four American warships, well armed with cannon, steamed into a port at the entrance of Yedo Bay. The commander, Commodore Matthew C. Perry, brought gifts from the President of the United States and a letter asking that Japanese ports be opened for trade and for the refueling of foreign vessels. The country was panic-stricken and so were the shogun and his court, for they were sensible enough to know that they could not fight against these ships. The letter was accepted; Perry said that he would return the next spring for the answer, and the "black ships" disappeared. When he came back the next February, a treaty was signed, opening two ports and allowing a foreign consul to live in Japan. As soon as this treaty was granted to the Americans, the Europeans came demanding the same rights, and could not be refused.

The opening of Japan and its incredibly quick conversion from a medieval country to a highly efficient modern one is a magnificent story. For ten or twelve years there was seething excitement. Violence broke out between those who wanted to drive out "the barbarians" and those who knew that it was impossible to do so and who, besides, longed to see the world and to do the very things that these barbarians were doing. The latter, of necessity, won, and the following events occurred.

In 1867 a boy of fourteen came to the throne, who proved to have both character and intelligence. He has gone down in history as the Emperor Meiji. In that same year the shogun resigned and his office was abolished, for it was clear that in this crisis there must be one government, not two. The next year the young emperor left Kyoto, where his ancestors had lived for a thousand years, and moved into the shogun's palace in Yedo, which was renamed Tokyo, or the eastern capital. A few months afterward, in the presence of his ministers, he took what is known as the Charter Oath, in which he promised that deliberative assemblies would be held, that the "uncivilized customs of former times" would be abandoned, and that "knowledge and wisdom shall be sought for in all quarters of the world." In this same momentous year Shinto was made the state religion, and all Buddhist images and symbols and their priests were removed from the Shinto shrines. A tremendous effort must be made by the whole people to meet the crisis, and only Shinto could unite and inspire them.

The willing resignation of the shogun while he was still in power was an extraordinary act. Others followed. In 1869 the four most powerful daimyo, who held vast lands on Kyushu, sent a document to the emperor offering him all their territory, their possessions, and their men. "The place where we live is the emperor's land," it said, "and the food that we eat is grown by the emperor's men. How can we make it our own?" The example of these men was soon followed, and two hundred and forty daimyo offered the emperor their lands and their revenues. This voluntary giving up of power and possessions has scarcely been equaled anywhere or at any time. The emperor now had not only the supreme power but also enough money to run the country. The daimyo were given one tenth of their former incomes, but they no longer had the great expense of maintaining their vast estates and households and supporting hundreds and sometimes thousands of samurai. The samurai were released from their service and had to seek other and unfamiliar occupations.

This series of events is known as the Meiji Restoration and the date given is 1868.

After the emperor's Charter Oath, hundreds of men were sent abroad to observe and to study, and hundreds of foreigners were invited to Japan to teach, to direct new industries, and to help the people to catch up with the most powerful and advanced nations. For as the Japanese looked out on the world, they found that the Spanish pilot's warning, three hundred years before, was a true one. Most of Asia had been conquered by the European nations, and they were now closing in on China, which was helpless before them.

The Japanese would not be conquered or helpless, nor would they be inferior to anyone on earth. Their pride and honor were touched to the quick. In order to defend themselves and to equal the Western nations, everything in the country had to be changed from top to bottom. A new government, universal education, mechanized industry in all its branches, and modern armaments must be introduced. This stupendous task was accomplished in one generation from the time of the Restoration. In 1895 Japan made war on China and easily defeated its old master. In 1905, with warships made in its own shipyards, it defeated Russia; it was the first Eastern nation to defeat a Western one. Success in war won the respect of the West, and Japan was accepted as an equal, one of the "great powers."

Shinto played an important part in this transformation. The work was done by a galaxy of brilliant young samurai, most of whom came from the great feudal domains of Kyushu. These were like small states, and they had been run by the samurai; on a modest scale, these men had experience in government. Now they gave themselves with single-hearted devotion to the service of their country. It was easy, not only for them, but for all the people to turn their loyalty from one province and a feudal lord to the whole beloved land and to the person of the young Emperor Meiji, who was proving himself worthy of his high station. The throne, the dynasty, "coeval with heaven and earth," was the inspiration for these amazing deeds. In a time of turmoil and change it was the one firm and unchanging element, the symbol of unity, the rock on which the new society was built. The unquestioning loyalty of the whole people came from the belief that the emperor was the direct descendant of Ama-terasu-O-mi-kami and that her descendants will continue to rule the land of the gods as long as heaven and earth endure. Whether everyone believed this, who can tell? But, in 1887, a cabinet minister came to Ise, the Sun Goddess's shrine, dressed in Western clothes and full of Western ideas. He trod with his hard shoes on consecrated ground and pushed aside with his cane a curtain beyond which no one was allowed to go. He was assassinated a few days later and his assassin became a popular hero; in fact he was considered a Kami.

A few decades later, Shinto was again invoked, falsely this time and for a deplorable purpose. Japan took its place in the modern world in an unhappy century, for less than ten years after its victory over Russia, World War I broke out. In the 1930's a clique of officers of the army and navy, with ministers who favored them, came into power. Wiser and more liberal men were assassinated or silenced by the police and by censorship, and the military men held all important government positions. (The same thing was happening at this time in Europe.) They undertook the disastrous venture of World War II, through which they proposed to set up a great empire in eastern Asia, ruled by Japan.

For this purpose and with the most modern weapons, these men invoked the ancient authority of Shinto. The Emperor Jimmu, according to tradition, had said, "The imperial rule shall be extended to all the cardinal points and the whole world shall be brought under one roof." The militarists took this saying as a slogan for their conquests: "All the world under one roof" justified their purpose. They also held that, since the remote ancestor of the emperors had been sent to earth by Ama-terasu, he alone was fit to rule the world.

It was a sad perversion of a faith that a Western scholar had once called "a religion of love and gratitude." By "the whole world" Jimmu had obviously meant the islands of Japan, which were all that he knew and which he was at that time laboriously conquering. The Sun Goddess had been quite definite about the country she was giving to her Sovran Grandchild: it was "The Plentiful Reed-Plains of Fifteen Thousand Autumns of Fresh Rice-Ears," that is, the same lovely islands.

The war ended in catastrophe and defeat. After the surrender, when Japan was occupied by the Allied Powers, one of their first orders was that Shinto must cease to be the state religion. The government must no longer support the shrines; Shinto doctrines must not be taught in public schools; no one must be required to take part in the rituals or to visit the shrines. The order was a very stern one and stated that its purpose was to wipe out the idea that the nation, its ruler, and its people were superior to any others and must therefore rule the world. Shortly afterward, on January 1, 1946, the emperor issued a proclamation about the reconstruction of the country, in which he said, "The bonds between us and our countrymen . . . do not originate in myth and legend. They do not have their basis in the fictitious idea that the emperor is a manifest god."

SHINTO TODAY

After 1945 Shinto became what it had been before the Restoration: a national but not a state religion. It is not supported by the government or taught in the public schools, but it is alive and active in a hundred thousand shrines and in the hearts of millions of people.

The most important of the shrines, the holy of holies, is that of the Sun Goddess at Ise, on the Shima peninsula on the southern shore of Honshu. It stands in a great park of tall evergreen trees which hide all the low buildings of unpainted, weathered wood until one is close to them. These trees remind an American immediately of redwoods; they are not nearly so tall, but they have the same straight, massive trunks, the same small branches that allow them to grow close together, and the same ancient dignity.

One enters the grounds of the shrine by a handsome, slightly arched bridge over a small river. At either end of the bridge there is a sacred gateway, a *torii,* which is made of two smoothed and rounded tree trunks joined near the top by a crossbeam; another beam lies across the top and projects beyond it and is often tilted up at both ends. A torii always marks the approach to a Shinto shrine. From

A close-up of the Shrine of the Sun Goddess at Ise. *(Consulate General of Japan, New York)*

the bridge one walks on a broad graveled path to the shore of the bright, shallow little river, where everyone dips his fingers and rinses his mouth with the water, as a ritual of purification. Then the curving path leads deeper into the silence and the beauty of the forest. Finally one comes to a flight of broad, stone steps that lead to a gateway in a solid wooden fence. The gate is open, but a white curtain hangs across it and beyond that no one may go except the high priests, the emperor, or his representatives. The worshiper bows before the curtain, claps his hands twice, says whatever prayer is in his heart, throws a coin on a cloth that is spread below the gate, and goes happily away.

The shrine itself is hidden behind three more fences and one sees no more than the top of its roof. Fortunately there are photographs of it. It is a small house, no larger than a fairly large room, like the very early shrines. It is raised from the ground on posts and has a balcony running around it reached by a flight of steps. It has a thickly thatched roof, cut very close and even at the edges. At each end the rafters are longer than the others and project in an X-shape above the point of the roof. A long beam lies between them resting on the cross of the X, and across this beam lie ten short logs to hold it down. The effect is solid, simple, archaic, and beautiful. There is no trace of Chinese or Buddhist influence. It is made of carefully chosen white wood, smoothed until it is like silk, but there is not a drop of paint or any decoration on it. Every twenty years it is taken down and a new shrine is built on an empty space adjoining it. The same pattern is used in thousands of shrines, large and small. Like the torii, the crossed rafters are the mark of a Shinto place of worship.

Inside this small building is believed to be the mirror that Ama-terasu gave to her August Grandson. It was kept in the royal palace until 92 B.C., when the emperor thought it would not be safe there. He entrusted it to his daughter and it was finally placed at Ise. It is not seen even by the emperor, for it is wrapped in layers of silk and placed in a box. A priestess is always in charge of the shrine, and she always belongs to the imperial family. At every large shrine there are also young girls, daughters of priests or of worthy citizens; they are dancers and musicians; they serve as secretaries or as attendants to honored guests. They dress in a white upper garment with loose flowing sleeves, and a long scarlet skirt; their black hair is tied at the nape of the neck and hangs down the back. They are not nuns or vestal virgins; when the time comes for them to marry, they leave and others take their place. The priests, too, are not monks; they marry and live with their families, wearing their white robes only when officiating at the shrine.

Three or four miles away, but in the same great forest, is the shrine of the Kami of Food, also a female figure. She is much honored and is closely associated with Amaterasu.

To these shrines, especially that of the Sun Goddess, millions of people come each year and at all times of the year. The great seasonal festivals are held there: the one in early spring when prayers for a good harvest are offered; the later one in June with prayers for the emperor, the nation, and the world; the offering of the first ripened grains of rice; the thanksgiving for the harvest in November, and still more. Besides the small hidden shrine, there are other buildings at Ise, which are open to everyone; there is one for religious ceremonies, a large one for sacred plays and dances and music. On great occasions a platform or pavilion is sometimes raised out of doors so that all may see and hear, for always the best dancers, actors, and musicians bring their skills to Ise.

At these times the emperor sends his representative

The Grand Festival of Toshiogu Shrine in Nikko. A palanquin is being carried at the left. *(Japan National Tourist Organization)*

with offerings, often lengths of cloth, reminiscent of those hung on the tree outside the goddess's cave. He does not come himself because, as high priest, he performs these rites in his own place of worship. There he has a copy of the mirror and of the sword of Susa-no-wo, which is in the shrine of Atsuta in the city of Nagoya; the original string of jewels is said to be in his possession. When any important event happens in the nation or to the imperial family, a messenger from the emperor reports it in the shrine at Ise; when the crown prince was married a few years ago, he and his bride went there themselves to announce their marriage.

Japan is a land of festivals, for Shinto is a happy faith. It celebrates life; its prayers are for the good things of this earthly life, and to assure them there must be a close communion with the divine powers. There is probably one festival or more, somewhere, every day of the year, for there are more well-known celebrations in a year than there are days, and innumerable small ones. Every shrine, however small, holds its own holiday at least once, and each occupation must worship and thank its protective deity. The occasions are therefore joyous ones.

The large shrines (Ise is an exception) usually stand in a wide enclosure where there are spacious courts, paved or graveled. Here, as well as in the buildings, plays and dances are held to entertain the Kami; some are stately and serious, like the Noh plays; some are comic; some, historical. There are jugglers and wrestling matches, horse races or archery contests, bonfires or boat races. Some festivals last for a day or for two or three days; some, like the great Gion celebration in Kyoto, last for a week. The whole population of that city (which was the imperial capital for a thousand years) takes part in it, and visitors come from all over the country to see it.

A feature of almost every such occasion is a procession, often a most spectacular one. The Kami rarely has an image—he is more a spirit than a person—but in every shrine there is a symbol of his presence. It is a very sacred object and, like the mirror of Ama-terasu, it is not seen even by the priests, for it is wrapped in silk and enclosed in a box. But at festive times the box is put into a palanquin and carried out in a procession, the priests leading and the people following. The palanquin is like a large chest and is usually elaborately carved, lacquered, and gilded; its domed cover has upcurling corners hung with silk tassels, and a gilded phoenix on top. It is set on horizontal poles and carried on the shoulders of strong young men. A small palanquin may be carried by four or eight men, but there are large ones that need twenty or thirty sturdy carriers. In small villages the purpose of the procession may be to bring the Kami's blessing to the fields or the seashore, or to show him his domain, or merely to give him pleasure.

In the great cities these pageants are a fine sight, for in addition to the palanquin there are huge floats, sometimes two or three stories high and surmounted by a spire. These are lavishly decorated, and riding on them are dancers and musicians; they are mounted on enormous wheels and drawn by dozens of men in handsome livery. They often carry figures that dramatize old stories or portray historic characters; this used to be done by actors, but now the figures are life-sized dolls. There are processions of warriors dressed in ancient costumes, or of men and women in the court dress of olden times. There is no end to the variety and splendor of these joyous festivals.

There are other holidays, celebrating the cherry blossoms and many other flowers in the spring, the iris and lotus in summer, the chrysanthemums and the bright leaves in autumn. There are Buddhist festivals, the most important being the three-day one in midsummer, when the spirits of the dead visit their families and their former homes, when every house hangs out its lantern to guide

Celebrating the Gion festival in Kyoto. *(Consulate General of Japan, New York)*

their steps and sends them away with the same soft, multitudinous lights. In addition to the many public festivities each Shinto family has a Kami-shelf in the house, where there are three objects of worship: a small shrine like that at Ise, in the center; the ancestral tablets on one side; and on the other, some indication of the local deity, the Uji-gami. Before these, offerings are made each day, and the local shrines are often visited for personal reasons. Beside the Kami-shelf there is often a Buddhist altar, for Buddhism has been restored to its old place and is a strong spiritual influence.

Most public celebrations are Shinto and in them is lasting proof of the value of the old traditions. Next to Ise in importance, on the opposite coast of Honshu, is the shrine of Izumo, where Susa-no-wo fought with the serpent and made his home. The present handsome building, of the same pattern as that at Ise, is believed to stand on the very site of the palace that was built for Susa-no-wo's descendant, who gave up the land to Ninigi-no-mikoto. His name is O-kuni-nushi, which means "great lord of the land," and he is much honored. On January 3 the emperor celebrates the descent of Ninigi; the accession and the death of the Emperor Jimmu are remembered in the shrine dedicated to him.

The great Gion festival in Kyoto is in honor of Susa-no-wo; many shrines pay homage to him, and his encounter with the serpent is a favorite subject for plays. These and innummerable other mythical and historical figures still live and play their parts in the life of Japan. The details of the ritual are also a reminder, especially of Ama-terasu's sojourn in the cave. The dances that the maidens perform, and which are now very decorous and stately, are in memory of the dance of the little goddess on the tub. In the silence of the forest of Ise one hears the shrill crowing of sacred cocks. A rice-straw rope, sometimes a foot thick in diameter, hangs across the door of every shrine and is used in many other ways; and pieces of paper cut in rectangular shapes are reminiscent of the offerings of cloth hung on the evergreen tree. Many other ceremonial details have their origin in the old tales.

To those people who believe that myths are an important part of the collective thinking of mankind, it is a joy to find them still vital and fresh in the life of a nation so modern and so efficient as Japan. But the great value of Shinto lies in its memory of the sources of our being, both earthly and spiritual. It insists that everyone should remember and live in harmony with these sources, in daily life and in acts of worship. The purpose of the many festivals is to draw people into communion with nature and with the Kami and consequently with one another. In many parts of the world there are hardly any communal celebrations left, and their loss is a sad one. Japan is one of the few civilized countries where they are still held, with joy and beauty.

On the temple bell
A butterfly,
Fast asleep.

—*Buson*

Notes

PART ONE: EAST AND WEST

1. Swami Abhedananda, *The Sayings of Ramakrishna* (New York, Vedanta Society, 1961), p.16.

PART TWO: HINDUISM

1. Bhágavad Gita, book VIII, 16–18.
2. Rig Veda, X, 129.
3. Kena Upanishad, I.
4. Isha Upanishad, 1–7 *passim.*
5. Chandogya Upanishad, VI, 1, 2, 8, 12.
6. Brihadaranyaka Upanishad, III, 9, 1.
7. Bhágavad Gita, book V, 23–25.
8. Katha Upanishad, II, 6, 10–11.
9. Bhágavad Gita, book II, 11–30 *passim.*
10. *Ibid.,* book XVIII, 8, 10, 41–49 *passim,* 61, 62.
11. Information about the life of Ramakrishna was obtained from the *Life of Sri Ramakrishna* (Calcutta, Advaita Ashrama, 1928).

12. Incidents and quotations from the life of Vínoba Bhave are from Hallam Tennyson, *India's Walking Saint* (Garden City, Doubleday and Company, 1955).

The poems on pages 46 and 55 are from *Songs of Kabir,* translated by Rabindranath Tagore (New York: Macmillan Company, 1915).

PART THREE: BUDDHISM

1. Dhammapada, chapters I, VIII, LX, X.
2. Majjhima Nikaya, III, 21. In Thomas W. Rhys Davids, trans., *Dialogues of the Buddha,* London, H. Frowde, 1899–1921.
3. Sutta Nipada, V, 148. In Thomas W. Rhys Davids, trans., *Buddhist Suttas,* Oxford, Clarendon Press, 1881.
4. The Larger Sukhavati Vyuha, XIX. In E. B. Cowell, editor, *Buddhist Mahayana Texts,* New York, Dover Publications, 1969, part II, pp. 41–42.

PART FOUR: THE RELIGION OF CHINA

1. Thomas Taylor Meadows, *The Chinese and Their Rebellions,* London, Smith, Elder and Company, 1856, p. 384.
2. Shu King (The Book of History), *The Chinese Classics,* part V, book I, section 2.
3. *Ibid.,* part II, book IV, section 1.
4. *Ibid.,* part IV, book VIII, section 1.
5. Li Ki (The Book of Rites), *The Chinese Classics,* book VII, section 4 *passim.*
6. Analects of Confucius, book VII, 1.
7. *Ibid,* book V, 9.
8. *Ibid.,* book XIX, 23 and 24.
9. *Ibid.,* book VII, 1.
10. *Ibid.,* book II, 4.
11. Doctrine of the Mean, XX, 18 ff., and XXII.
12. Analects of Confucius, book XIV, 30.
13. The quotations on the following pages are from the *Tao Teh Ching* (or *King*) by Lao-tse. Many translations have been made of this book; the writer has used several different ones. See "Books for Further Reading."
14. G. Willoughby-Meade, *Chinese Ghouls and Goblins,* New York, Stokes, 1926, pp. 17–18.

15. Valentine R. Burkhardt, *Chinese Creeds and Customs,* Hong Kong, South China Morning Post, 1956, p. 51.
16. G. Willoughby-Meade, *op. cit.*, pp.130–131.
17. *Ibid.,* pp. 51–52.
18. Alan Watts, *The Way of Zen* (Vintage Books, 1956), pp. 89–90.

The poem on page 103 is from *The Book of Songs,* translated by Arthur Waley (New York: Grove Press, 1960). The poems on pages 138 and 155 are from *The Lost Flute,* edited by T. Fisher (London: Unwin, 1923). The poem on page 147 is from *Zen Flesh, Zen Bones: A Collection of Zen and Pre-Zen Writings,* compiled by Paul Reps (Garden City: Doubleday and Company, Anchor Book).

PART FIVE: SHINTO, THE WAY OF THE GODS

1. The stories on pp. 154–165 are retold, not quoted, from the two early scriptures of Shinto: the Kojiki and the Nihongi. The Kojiki was translated by Basil Hall Chamberlain (J. L. Thompson and Company, 1932). The Nihongi was translated by William George Aston (Kegan, Paul, 1896).
2. Joseph W. T. Mason, *The Meaning of Shinto* (New York, E. P. Dutton, 1935), p. 160.
3. William George Aston, *The Way of the Gods* (London, Longmans, Green, 1905), pp. 281–284.
4. *Ibid.,* pp. 301–302.

The poem on page 157 is from *Sources of Japanese Tradition,* edited by William Theodore de Bary (New York: Columbia University Press, 1958). The poem on page 178 is from *Zen Flesh, Zen Bones: A Collection of Zen and Pre-Zen Writings,* compiled by Paul Reps (Garden City: Doubleday and Company, Anchor Book).

Books for Further Reading

In recent years many excellent books have been written about Eastern religions and every aspect of Eastern cultures. Many of these are available in paperback. The reader is advised to go, if possible, to a large bookstore and to make his own choice. The following books are recommended. Unless hardcover is stated, all books listed are in paperback.

TEXTS OF HINDUISM

Arnold, Sir Edward, translator, *The Song Celestial* (the Bhágavad Gita). Wheaton, Illinois: Theosophical Publishing House, 1970.

MacNicol, Nicol, editor, *Hindu Scriptures.* New York: E. P. Dutton, 1938. Hardcover.

Mascaró, Juan, translator, *The Bhágavad Gita.* Baltimore: Penguin Books, 1962.

Prabhavananda, Swami, and Manchester, Frederick, translators, *The Upanishads.* New York: New American Library.

Seeger, Elizabeth, *The Five Sons of King Pandu; Story of the*

Máhabhárata. Reading, Massachusetts: Addison Wesley Company, 1967. Hardcover

———, *The Ramáyana.* Reading, Massachusetts: Addison Wesley, 1969. These books tell the complete stories (much abridged) of the two epics. Hardcover

BOOKS ABOUT HINDUISM

Abhedananda, Swami, *The Sayings of Ramakrishna.* New York: Vedanta Society, 1961. Hardcover

Fischer, Louis, *Life of Mahatma Gandhi.* New York: Macmillan Company, 1962.

Radhakrishnan, S., *The Hindu View of Life.* New York: Macmillan Company, 1962.

Sen, K. M., *Hinduism.* Baltimore: Penguin Books, 1961.

Shastri, H. P., *Yoga.* New York: Crown Publishers, Inc., 1960.

Spiegelberg, Frederic, *Spiritual Practices of India.* New York: Citadel Press, 1962.

Tennyson, Hallam, *India's Walking Saint.* Garden City: Doubleday and Company, 1955. Hardcover

TEXTS OF BUDDHISM

Babbitt, Irving, translator, *Dhammapada.* Philadelphia: J. B. Lippincott Company, 1965.

Cowell, E. B., Editor, *Buddhist Mahayana Texts.* New York: Dover Publications, 1969.

Narada, Thera, translator, *Dhammapada.* New York: Paragon Book Reprint Corporation, 1954.

Warren, Henry Clarke, editor, *Buddhism in Translation.* New York: Atheneum Publishers, 1963. Contains many valuable excerpts from various Buddhist scriptures.

BOOKS ABOUT BUDDHISM

Carus, Paul, *The Gospel of Buddha.* Chicago: Open Court, 1917.

Chang, Garma C. C., *The Practice of Zen.* New York: Perennial Library, Harper and Row, 1970. The author is a Chinese Zen Master.

Humphreys, Christmas, *Buddhism.* Baltimore: Penguin Books, 1967.

Suzuki, Beatrice L., *Mahayana Buddhism.* New York: Macmillan Company, 1969. A clear exposition of a complicated subject.

Thomas, Edward Joseph, *Life of Buddha.* New York: Barnes and Noble, 1956.

Warren, Henry Clarke, *Everyman's Life of Buddha.* Conesville, Iowa: John Westbury.

Watts, Alan, *The Way of Zen.* New York: Vintage Books, 1956.

Zen Buddhism. New York: Peter Pauper Press, 1959.

TEXTS OF CONFUCIANISM AND TAOISM

All the Chinese Classics can be found in the Sacred Books of the East series (James Legge, translator). Oxford: Clarendon Press, 1879–1910.

The I-Ching, or Book of Changes, should be read in the translation by Richard Wilhelm, with an introduction by C. G. Jung. New York: Pantheon Books, Bollingen Series XIX, 1950.

Lin Yu-tang, translator, *The Wisdom of Laotse.* New York: Modern Library, 1948. With valuable notes. Hardcover.

MacHovec, F. J. translator, *The Book of Tao.* New York: Peter Pauper Press, 1962.

Waley, Arthur, translator, *The Analects of Confucius.* New York: Random House.

———, *The Book of Songs* (one of the Chinese Classics). New York: Grove Press, 1960.

Ware, James R., translator, *The Sayings of Chuang Chou.* New York: Mentor Books, 1963. A delightful book that reveals the subtlety and humor of the Chinese philosophers.

BOOKS ABOUT CHINESE RELIGION

Creel, Herrlee Glessner, *Confucius and the Chinese Way.* New York: Harper, 1960.

Waley, Arthur, editor, *Three Ways of Thought in Ancient China.* New York: Doubleday Anchor Books.

TEXTS OF SHINTO

Aston, William George, translator, *Nihongi, Chronicles of Japan.* London: Kegan, Paul, 1896.

Chamberlain, Basil Hall, translator, *Kojiki* (the ancient chronicles and mythology). London: J. L. Thompson and Company, 1932.

Philippi, Donald L., translator, *Norito.* Tokyo: Institute of Japanese Culture and Classics, 1959. Hardcover

BOOKS ABOUT SHINTO

Aston, William George, *Shinto, the Ancient Religion of Japan.* London: Constable, 1907. Hardcover, available only in libraries

Bauer, Helen, and Carlquist, Sherwin, *Japanese Festivals.* New York: Doubleday and Company, 1965. A delightful book with many photographs. Hardcover

Herbert, Jean, *Shinto, The Fountainhead of Japan.* Translated from the French "Aux Sources du Japon: le Shinto." New York: Stein and Day, 1967. For anyone seriously interested in Shinto, this is an excellent and thorough book. Hardcover

Holtom, Daniel Clarence, *The National Faith of Japan.* London: Kegan, Paul, 1938. Hardcover

Ono, Sokyo, *Shinto, the Kami Way.* Rutland, Vermont: Charles E. Tuttle Company, 1962.

Index

(An asterisk after a page number refers to an illustration.)

About the Author

Elizabeth Seeger has written five books on various aspects of Eastern history, literature, and philosophy. The first one, *The Pageant of Chinese History,* was written to implement a course in Oriental history that she introduced into the curriculum of the progressive Dalton School in New York City. Among her other books are superb retellings for young and adult readers of the Indian epics, the *Mahabhárata* and the *Ramáyana.*

Miss Seeger, who has always believed that we should know far more than we do about the cultures of Asia, was associated with the Dalton School for over thirty-five years, first as a teacher and then as an administrator. Nowadays, when she is not writing, she occasionally draws portraits. Her home is in Bridgewater, Connecticut.

YA
294 Seeger, Elizabeth
SEE Eastern religions